SUE THE
MESSENGER

SUE THE
MESSENGER

How legal harassment by corporates is shackling
reportage and undermining democracy in India

SUBIR GHOSH

with

PARANJOY GUHA THAKURTA

PARANJOY

First published in India in 2016 by:
Paranjoy Guha Thakurta
paranjoy@gmail.com

ISBN: 978-1533078612

Publishing facilitation: AuthorsUpFront

For all those who have stood by me,
through thick and thin, unconditionally so

Contents

Introduction

The summer had not yet reached a boil that mid-April afternoon of 2014, when on our way to the Press Club of India nestled in the heart of capital New Delhi, we learnt that lawyers for Reliance Industries Limited (RIL) and its chairman and managing director Mukesh Ambani had shot off a legal notice to us.

The notice of 16 April 2014 alleged defamation, thought of a nearly-600 page tome as a 'pamphlet', called for a cease on the sale, publication and distribution of the book, suggested that all existing copies be destroyed, that online publicity be stopped, and an unconditional apology be tendered by us. The book in question was *Gas Wars: Crony Capitalism and the Ambanis,* that had been officially launched the previous evening at a heavily-attended event at the cultural hub, India Habitat Centre. And the 'we' were the authors of this book, who had co-authored *Gas Wars* with Jyotirmoy Chaudhuri. The book had been unofficially released on the last day of the previous month, and had been in circulation for a fortnight.

The same notice, as it transpired in due course, was also sent to our publishing facilitator Authors UpFront, distributor FEEL Books, the printer, Internet retailers Amazon, Flipkart and Kobo, and of all people even Deepshikha Shankar, who was working with the Delhi-based Foundation for Media Professionals (FMP) and had forwarded an electronic invitation for the launch function to people on her mailing list.

A week later, on 22 April, we received a second legal notice—this one from lawyers representing Anil Ambani and the conglomerate he headed, Anil Dhirubhai Ambani Group (ADAG). It unequivocally asked for the removal of the website promoting the book, gaswars.in, besides bringing an immediate halt to the sale, publication, distribution and circulation of *Gas Wars*.

Both notices, scripted in standard and prosaic legalese, said that 'failing compliance' their clients would be 'constrained to adopt such civil and/or criminal proceedings' as 'advised.'

The following day, all nine respondents of the first notice from Khaitan & Co received another round of notices expressing unhappiness at the proceedings of the launch event. This notice took umbrage at lead author Paranjoy Guha Thakurta quoting former West Bengal Governor Gopal Krishna Gandhi during the 15 April launch function. Gandhi had described RIL as a 'parallel state' exemplifying corporate greed, earlier that very morning at the Indian government's auditorium in the capital—Vigyan Bhavan. Gandhi made his remarks while delivering the 15th DP Kohli Memorial lecture, titled 'Eclipse at Noon: Shadows over India's Conscience', organised on the occasion of the conclusion of the golden jubilee celebrations of the country's premier police agency, the Central Bureau of Investigation (CBI).

The third notice came with a veneer of undisguised intimidation: we were asked to cough up 'token damages of ₹100 crore' within ten days. We later learnt that a similar notice had been served on the editor of *MoneyLife* magazine and moneylife.in website, Sucheta Dalal for publishing a review of *Gas Wars*. On 23 May, a fourth notice was received by our lawyer from Khaitan & Co reiterating the views that had been already made about RIL's misgivings on our book.

The notices from RIL's lawyers claimed that we had defamed India's richest man by describing him as an 'oligarch' and stating that he and his brother were 'greedy and vengeful' when they fought over the allocation of a natural resource (natural gas) that is supposed to belong to the people of India. They suggested that the lead author was an 'interested party' since he was on the governing council of Common Cause, which was among the litigants in a case in the Supreme Court against RIL and the government, a fact that had been categorically disclosed in *Gas Wars*. The notices said it was defamatory on our part to have suggested that RIL and the Ambanis had put 'pressure' on the Congress-led United Progressive Alliance (UPA) government to change ministerial portfolios to suit RIL's convenience.

Our point was, and is even now, crystal clear: if anyone should be complaining it ought to be former Prime Minister Manmohan Singh. After all, he was the head of the government at the time and it was his unfettered prerogative to decide who held which ministerial portfolio. Significantly, the notices did not point out a single factual error in what had been published and also not conceded that the company's versions on the different controversies surrounding the pricing and utilisation of KG gas had been fleshed out in elaborate detail. An entire section in the appendix had been devoted to RIL's perception and understanding of the controversy.

RIL's version of the story had been outlined explicitly and meticulously in the main text, and there had been no earth-shattering revelation in *Gas Wars*. Much of the information provided in the book—from the assertions made by the Comptroller and Auditor-General (CAG) of India to what had arguably led the two Ambani brothers to first part ways, and then engage in a long-drawn legal battle over the supply of natural gas from the Krishna-Godavari basin—had long been in the public domain, and discussed by all and sundry. The saga itself had played out over more than a decade, and all that we had done was stitch disparate elements together, and present all that in a contextual manner for the ordinary reader.

The last bit therein was one of the reasons why we had decided to put everything together in the form of a book. Along the way, we picked up and published some factual information that had hitherto not been in the public domain. Such information included the last interview given by Subir Raha, former chairman of the Oil and Natural Gas Corporation (ONGC), on the battle between the Ambani brothers, and former minister for petroleum Mani Shankar Aiyar describing his own government's decision to increase the administered price of natural gas as an instance of a 'fraud' being committed on the country.

It is pertinent to mention this here since all the time that we were working on the project, as also post-publication, we had been asked time and again: why would you folks want to take on the (powerful) Ambanis? No, it was never a question of 'taking on' the Ambanis—that would suggest we had nothing better to do in life. What lay in front of us was a beguiling story that had unfolded at a tortuous pace over more than ten years. Everything had been reported and analysed in varying detail by scores of scribes and writers. What was left to be done was to contextualise the intrigues, and paint the big picture.

That's all we did: paint the big picture. There was a story out there, and it was crying to be told. As hard-boiled journalists, it would have been self-defeating for us to let it go. We had done what journalists are supposed to do—tell the story to the citizenry. Of course, this could not have been done in the form of a series of 1,000-word articles in a newspaper, magazine or website. It had to take the form of a book.

The book made news, soon enough. But not in the way that authors usually want—booming sales and flattering reviews. There were neither favourable nor negative reviews in the mainstream media; all that appeared sparingly were news about us being served legal notices, most of them tersely-worded single-column pieces buried deep inside the pages. It was as if the narrative about two of India's wealthiest men did not exist at all in the mainstream media—it had been swallowed up by the fabled news hole.

It has been more than two years since *Gas Wars* was launched in April 2014, and we have often been asked: what happened to your case? The answer is simple: there never was any legal case; there had been just those four notices. Contrary to what some may presume, Khaitan & Co, representing Mukesh Ambani and RIL, and Mulla & Mulla & Craigie Blunt & Caroe, representing Anil Ambani and ADAG, did not file legal proceedings against either us or any of our associates in any court of law in India or anywhere else, since legal notices were served on us during the politically-surcharged summer of 2014.

But, it was not the still-developing, snail-paced KG gas story that set us thinking beyond *Gas Wars*; it was the notices. Now, there's a term, one that has been gaining currency worldwide, to denote the impact such legal notices have not only on those on whom these have been served, but on others too. It's called 'chilling effect'. In legal jargon, such notices are called SLAPPs, or strategic lawsuits against public participation—that is, litigation meant to harass, intimidate and silence critical writers who are expected to give in after they are faced with prospects of incurring high expenditure on legal defence. The chilling effect is applicable to others as well—it is meant to silence not just the people in question, but also others who might wish to speak or write on the subject. Nipping things in the dissenting bud, if you please.

We knew we had been SLAPPed, but we did not miss what had been already happening around us, and what emerged in the months to come. Three months before the *Gas Wars* launch, in January 2014, had come the appalling news that publishers Bloomsbury had withdrawn and shockingly pulped copies of *The Descent of Air India*, chronicled by Jitender Bhargava, a former executive director of the airline. The book was originally released on 11 October 2013, and a criminal defamation suit filed against the author and publisher in November by a lawyer representing former Union civil aviation minister Praful Patel of the Nationalist Congress Party (NCP). Among other things, Bhargava's book had alleged that Patel was aware of Air India's shrinking marketing share, and yet gave bilateral rights to foreign airlines.[1]

Around the same time, a harried Tamal Bandopadhyay was negotiating a December 2013 legal hurdle propped up in the form of a ₹200 crore defamation suit filed by the Sahara India Pariwar in the Calcutta High Court over his book *Sahara: The Untold Story*. Publisher Jaico too had been targeted. After months of parleys, both parties reached an out-of-court settlement following which the book carried a disclaimer by Sahara which claimed, among other things, that the book contained 'defamatory content'.

---

1   Jitender Bhargava self-published an enlarged version of *The Descent of Air India* in early 2016; and the case was still on when this book was being readied for printing. The metropolitan magistrate hearing the case on 5 November 2015, while denying any further adjournment, passed an order listing the case for final hearing on 28 January 2016. When the court met that day, Praful Patel's lawyer sought yet another adjournment, which the judge declined. The judge after admonishing the lawyer and reiterating that too many adjournments had already been granted imposed a penalty of ₹3,000 on Patel.

The story of the three books was summed up by journalist Salil Tripathi in *Caravan* magazine in September 2014:

> It is in the public interest to scrutinise how these companies are run. Whether Reliance is squatting on gas reserves and refusing to increase production unless the government agrees to a particular price; whether Sahara's millions of depositors are real people or phantoms legitimising someone's parallel income; and whether the national carrier's efforts to grow are stymied by vested interests cannot be the concerns of only the institutions under scrutiny. By attempting to force such books out of the public domain, businesses and politicians perpetuate the impression that they have something to hide. And, to further warp the debate, they may even provide the halo of martyrdom to authors whose books would otherwise not have been widely noticed.

> At stake here is not only freedom of expression, but also readers' and investors' right to know, and the principle of the free flow of market-sensitive information. Companies have the legal obligation to protect shareholder value (which would suffer if a book makes damaging claims against the company) but the more important question is that of whose interests are actually served by these lawsuits—shareholders' or company promoters'?

Tripathi, also a senior advisor on global issues with the London-based Institute for Human Rights and Business (IHRB), echoed our exact sentiments when he concluded:

> Markets thrive on information, not secrecy. By threatening journalists and writers, companies tilt the playing field heavily to their advantage. Courts that see such lawsuits purely in terms of a businessman's reputation, and not the wider public interest, do a huge disservice to the markets, and to society at large. The time for India to overhaul its laws on defamation is now, and

not just because of religious hotheads threatening to burn books they don't like.

In an ideal world, more writers should want to write more detailed books that dramatise and humanise business so that society better understands how business decisions affect people's lives. What prevents such writing is not only businessmen's reclusiveness or the complexity of their relationships with politicians, but the ever present threat of billion-rupee lawsuits. Changing that will require companies, the government and the judiciary to better understand the public interest. Without a sword hanging over their heads, writers will write more clearly, let information flow more freely, make markets more efficient and deliver well-paced yarns that draw into the conversation on the national economy even those who switch channels as soon as the graphs with stock prices appear on the nightly news.

In the interregnum, the darling of the Indian Fourth Estate— Infosys Limited, that had always benefited from an indulgent media coverage—slapped defamation notices collectively on three newspapers and journalists claiming damages of ₹2,000 crore for 'loss and reputation and goodwill due to circulation of defamatory articles.' The newspapers—*Economic Times, Times of India* and *Financial Express*—were given 24 hours to remove articles from their websites and other media, and issue an unconditional apology.

It was time to sit up and take notice. The question of intolerance, that cleaved Indian society down the middle in the second half of 2015 and exacerbated in the first quarter of 2016, was already rife in the minds of those working on the issues of defamation and SLAPPs. What was earlier intermittent, was now increasingly taking the shape of a distinct trend in the targeting of writers and journalists.

At at time when corporatisation of the media in the country is virtually complete and there is increased hounding of organisations and individuals for their perceived political and social dissent, there are still dauntless journalists and percipient writers who work overtime to bring to readers riveting and incisive stories that delve far deeper than the mundane and insipid headlines. And then, there are stories that in themselves merit a larger canvas on which to be told. Such writers and journalists, by virtue of the very work itself, have to write or report about corporates, and the end-product (be it a long-form feature or an exhaustive book) is hardly ever the subservient hagiography that corporates usually look forward to in business reporting. While more writers and journalists are increasingly writing about corporate corruption and crony capitalism, it is also being increasingly seen that corporates have been intimidating writers and journalists with, what are described as, SLAPP suits.

This is a matter of concern, especially since most scams and scandals that have rocked both the country and its Parliament since 2010 have had corporates figuring as either the beneficiaries, or at least definitely in the murky cast of unsavoury characters. Corruption involving corporate houses range from simple money laundering and accumulation/flight of black money to gross violations of both environmental and corporate laws. One cannot talk of weeding out corruption, by turning a blind eye to the roles and activities of (many) corporate houses. This is where writing about corporations assumes significance: if one is obstructed from writing/reporting about corporate houses, not only is that an act of aggression against press freedom, it is also an act that undermines democracy, by depriving the public of the right to know.

That is what this book too, like *Gas Wars*, seeks to do: paint the big picture. This work does not purport to be a veritable and comprehensive catalogue of defamation cases or SLAPP suits filed in India; and, nor does it want to come across as an academic treatise on the subject. It is a collection of stories about stories.

— Subir Ghosh

I

The Unhappy Prince

Biographies of Indian businessmen hitherto had been unabashed hagiographies that would be steeped in eulogistic verbiage and obsequious idiom. Most of these accounts would have been commissioned works—either by the businessmen themselves, or by the companies they would have set up. The writers would ask no uncomfortable questions of the businessmen, and the kowtowing biographies would be overflowing with unadulterated adulation. The history of Indian business writing might have remained so had it not been for a no-nonsense reporter for the Hong Kong-based news magazine *Far Eastern Economic Review* (FEER), who was posted in India towards the fag end of 1990.

The reporter was Hamish McDonald, an Australian who had written an unflattering account of Indonesian strongman Suharto ten years earlier. *Suharto's Indonesia* explained how the former Indonesian military ruler's tortured upbringing made him incapable of reining in his family's corrupt dealings. The book, published in January 1980, was a captivating collection of first-hand impressions and accounts seamed together from his stay in Jakarta between 1975 and 1978, when he freelanced for the *Sydney Morning Herald, Washington Post* and *Financial Times*.

McDonald was well-versed with turmoil, and possessed the hard-nosed reporter's penchant for sniffing out news. New Delhi, in that smoggy December of 1990, was certainly in turmoil, or at least the political climate was. Chandra Shekhar had only the previous month pulled the rug from under the feet of the Janata Dal-led National Front ministry of Vishwanath Pratap Singh, and become Prime Minister of the breakaway Samajwadi Janata Party (SJP)-led government supported from the outside by the Congress. Economic reforms were yet to be heard of, secessionist militancy was on an ascendancy in Kashmir, and the United Liberation Front of Asom (ULFA) was running a parallel administration in Assam. The country was at a cusp, and it was an opportune time for a journalist to land in India.

The weekly FEER covered politics, business, economics, technology, social and cultural issues throughout Asia, but focused on Southeast Asia and Greater China; McDonald was therefore here to do stories that delved beyond the headlines for a non-Indian readership. The political turbulence and uncertainty in India provided only a happening backdrop; the discerning eye of the FEER's South Asia bureau chief sifted through the political clutter and hovered around a businessman: Dhirubhai Ambani, founder of Reliance Industries Limited (RIL). The meteoric rise and the unmistakable clout of Ambani struck McDonald's journalistic fancy: 'Dhirubhai Ambani embodied all of the revolutionary capitalism that sympathetic and impatient analysts within the Western paradigm believed was lurking inside the Indian economy, pressing to be released from bureaucracy.'

Only the following month after landing in Delhi, McDonald attended the wedding of Dhirubhai's younger son, Anil. The interaction mattered to both sides—McDonald was looking for that upbeat business story, and the ambitious Reliance, planning to expand beyond the uninspiring Indian shores, needed favourable mileage in a foreign magazine. For Reliance Industries, this would be nothing short of a public relations exercise. An exclusive with the Ambani patriarch materialised the next month, and the FEER journalist soon had a sprawling cover story which 'portrayed Ambani as the business underdog trying to break through the government's red tape and the prejudices of a tired Bombay (Mumbai) business establishment.'

It all went 'swimmingly', as McDonald remembered. 'Tony Jesudasan (a key Reliance executive and aide of Dhirubhai's younger son Anil Ambani) would ring me and feed me with bits of news. I was in that kind of circle, 'Reliance friends', I guess.'

Reliance Industries wanted to showcase itself as the modern corporation as opposed to the old family firms established in colonial times or those that had prospered in the 1950s after Independence during the Licence Raj—an era when elaborate licences and regulations had to be negotiated to set up businesses— and had passed on the company leadership to the second and third generations. What went unsaid or was muttered only in hushed tones was that Reliance too had made the best of the Licence Raj by having rules bent and regulations twisted to suit its business interests.

The Reliance story had McDonald in its grip then on. 'I guess I was sucked in a bit. It was of course a good story. It was the usual story, you know—that of the amazing tycoon who inspired the share ownership among the emerging Indian middle class, who managed to keep his share prices and dividends rising, who amazingly, through these years had held meetings in football stadiums, and was kind of a rock star of the corporate world,' McDonald was to say of the Ambani czar.

McDonald's relations with Reliance remained cordial, even

as the company gradually started growing bigger on foreign
shores with the era of liberalisation being ushered from June
1991 onwards by the PV Narasimha Rao government, especially
finance minister Manmohan Singh, the unrepentant advocate
of economic reforms. McDonald needed a bigger canvas to tell
both the story of Ambani and the interface between business and
politics; the idea of a book to do this fleetingly crossed his mind
in 1992. He shared his thoughts at his second meeting with
Ambani, who was 'receptive' to the idea and felt that his story
would indeed be an inspiration for younger Indians. McDonald
agreed to bounce the final draft of the manuscript off Ambani,
and the understanding was that the former would retain the right
of final say.

But life has its own way of making course corrections. Towards
the end of 1993, there were rumours of government tenders being
rigged in favour of Reliance Industries for the awarding of contracts
for oil exploration in the Arabian Sea. McDonald faced a difficult
choice at hand—write about what was being seen as a 'one-horse
race,' or soft-pedal on the issue since he needed cooperation from
the family and the company for the book. The reporter decided
that his loyalties at the end of the day lay with the magazine he
worked for, and wrote diligently on the Panna-Mukta oilfields and
Tapti gas fields in the offshore Mumbai basin off India's west coast.
The first of the two articles prompted Anil Ambani to describe it
as 'defamatory;' not in the form of a legal notice, but in a cribbing
letter to the head of Australian resources giant BHP (Broken Hill
Proprietary, now the British-Australian company, BHP-Billiton),[2]
with copies marked to the heads of the Australian and American

---

2   BHP Billiton was created in 2001 through the merger of the Australian
     Broken Hill Proprietary Company Limited (BHP) and the Anglo–Dutch
     Billiton plc.

diplomatic missions in New Delhi. The journalist's relations with the Ambanis thereafter soured.

The oil exploration ventures of Reliance Industries were mired in controversy from the start. In 1991, the cash-strapped Indian government had invited private sector participation in the oil and gas sector. Under the new policy, the government allowed the state-owned Oil and Natural Gas Corporation (ONGC) to enter into joint ventures with private parties. The public sector unit had explored huge tracts of oil and gas fields in offshore India, which included the Krishna-Godavari gas basin off the coast of Andhra Pradesh. Going a step further, the government also leased out oil and gas fields already discovered and developed by ONGC to joint ventures clobbered together for this very purpose. In August 1992, the ministry of petroleum and natural gas invited bids for the further development of the Panna-Mukta oil fields, setting the last date for receiving tenders at 31 December 1992.

Reliance Industries, together with Enron, entered the fray and the other big contender was the Australian resources giant BHP, which pitched for the ONGC leases in partnership with the Tata group. Accusations were levelled by rival bidders insisting that tenders were being rigged in favour of Reliance Industries. McDonald investigated the allegations on his own, and reported that BHP representatives told him in turn that they found it difficult to compete in an environment where the specifications were being changed at the last minute, possibly to ease the way for RIL to grab the lucrative deals. On 31 March 1993, the government retrospectively extended the last date for receipt of the bids. In October 1993, a committee of secretaries from the finance, revenue and petroleum departments/ministries awarded the Panna-Mukta oilfield. Enron and Reliance Industries each held

30 per cent and ONGC retained 40 per cent. Incidentally, Enron's share was bought over by British Gas in 2002.

Soon after he began investigating the story, McDonald 'got a summons' for a meeting with Anil Ambani who 'was very testy.' Anil alleged that the Australian journalist was tacitly assisting the BHP officials in town. 'Wish I was, he (the BHP official) is Australian you know and we could show each other around the place,' said McDonald now, with a tinge of sarcasm. 'I started falling off the drip feed after that and I think they regarded me as no longer a friend.'

McDonald, meanwhile, stepped up work on his book; and physical work it was since he put in a considerable amount of legwork. From darting through the nooks and crannies of Bombay to running around several cities in Gujarat and distant London, he tried to re-trace the footprints of Dhirubhai Ambani. He started where the businessman himself had—in Chorwad, literally meaning 'Settlement of Thieves', and then in nearby Junagadh. He spoke to Dhirubhai's contemporaries, and wrote in elaborate detail about how this youngster in November 1947 had resolutely stood up to a police officer who had mistakenly apprehended activists of the Junagadh Vidyarthi Samiti who had gone to an area to protect shops belonging to Muslims from being looted by marauding Hindi rioters in a post-Independence surcharged atmosphere. Dhirubhai Ambani was a man of guts, no doubt.

The discomfiture in the Indian business world nevertheless was pronounced—they all wanted to know if the book was to be an authorised biography. For, if it wasn't, none wanted to be quoted out of turn, and earn the wrath of Ambani. Still, there were some others who sought a clearance on being quoted from Dhirubhai Ambani himself, only to be given the cold shoulder. In July 1995,

McDonald quit his job at FEER[3] to devote full time to the book. He would shuttle between New Delhi and hometown Sydney—work in India for a couple of months, and fly back home to put his thoughts together and pen them down. He was in no tearing hurry, and in no mood to do a rush job.

All this while, his work was an open secret, and Reliance Industries public relations executives even met him to enquire about what he was working on, and his unannounced intentions. 'All the Reliance flacks—Tony Jesudasan, Yogesh Desai, Jacob John and Deepak Neogi and others in Mumbai—were furiously taking me out to lunch on account of what I had in mind. I played it straight and said that it would not be a hatchet job but a fair review, but received no commitment,' said McDonald. The Australian journalist, meanwhile, remained suspect in view of his earlier reportage on the oilfield contracts.

'Some of Dhirubhai's old mates were telling me stories about his early days and colourful stories, getting arrested and cargo seized, bogus shipments of exports to get the credit. He would import polyester fibre and all that stuff. A picture of a prankster turned manipulator. This carried on, people started talking to me, the Aden people, the Gujarat employees and the early chapters were building up, the best chapters really. It all came to a grinding halt at the end of 1996.'

Yet, it was in early 1996 that an incident had made it amply clear that McDonald had been 'cut off' and that he was effectively 'on his own.' In January, he flew over to Mumbai to interview one of Dhirubhai Ambani's 'key cronies,' Ratibhai Muchhala, who had studied with Ambani in Junagadh and had been export manager

3　The Hong Kong-based *Far Eastern Economic Review* was originally a weekly. Due to financial difficulties, it converted to a monthly in December 2004. FEER printed its final issue in December 2009.

for the magnate for decades, handling textile exports through the Gujarati diaspora in East Africa, the Middle East and later the United Kingdom.

Muchhala operated from an office in the industrial belt behind the Santa Cruz airport. Even though he had agreed to the interview, McDonald met a 'very embarrassed secretary' who said that Muchhala was not there, but was at the Reliance Industries head office instead. Dhirubhai's office had advised him not to meet the writer. He instead was put through to Dinesh Sheth, Dhirubhai's personal assistant who was 'very sheepish' and said that the tycoon 'would prefer that this project did not go ahead.' McDonald was told that there were many others who wanted to write a biography of Dhirubhai, but the latter had indicated that he did not want to encourage or cooperate on a biography at that time.

Regardless, there obviously were some others who opened up. Among McDonald's key sources was the 'wonderful old businessman' Jamnadas Moorjani. This affable man turned out to be a 'fountain of knowledge' on the Indian textiles industry; his office in a back lane in the Kalbadevi area was a favourite source of news and tip-offs for journalists. Moorjani, who died in December 2000, headed the All-India Crimpers Association from 1978 to 1982 and had been witness to the savage face-off over polyester control between Dhirubhai and Nusli Wadia, the Parsi businessman who owned Bombay Dyeing, a textiles brand from the Wadia Group. Wadia used dimethyl terepthalate (DMT), a feedstock used in manufacturing polyester yarn, while Ambani was a fierce advocate of purified terephthalic acid (PTA).

The *Indian Express,* owned by Ramnath Goenka and edited by Arun Shourie, became an ally of Wadia and published a series of exposes on duty evasion by Reliance Industries through under-invoicing that were researched and authored by Goenka's chartered accountant, S Gurumurthy, who later went on to become the co-convenor of the Swadeshi Jagaran Manch (SJM), the economic front of the Sangh Parivar. Moorjani himself had led a campaign by independent polyester texturisers against a duty hike in yarn in November 1982 allegedly engineered by Ambani. Sometime in 1986, Moorjani was attacked by a knife-wielding gang as he was leaving his Kalbadevi office, and he almost lost an arm. Though there were conjectures that this was a result of the business war, no link was ever established.

McDonald was briefed in considerable detail by Wadia, who shared 'his side of the battle.' One Friday, at 5 in the evening, Wadia asked him to reach his office in the Fort area of Mumbai. Wadia was in a talkative mood, and the two spoke for over five hours. 'When we eventually packed up, the building was empty. Wadia himself went to the door and let us out. I rushed back to the hotel, sat for hours, and put it down while it was fresh in my mind,' said McDonald, on how he put the fragments together.

It was not only Ambani's colleagues and rivals who were reticent or circumspect on speaking up, or even speaking about— former Prime Minister Vishwanath Pratap Singh too skirted the request for an interview on the pretext that he could not talk about a specific company. There was a reason for McDonald to look at Singh. It was the VP Singh government, unlike the two Congress ministries preceding his 343-day tenure, which had been firm with Ambani's Reliance Industries. Singh, as a vigilante finance minister from 1984 to 1987 in the Rajiv Gandhi government, had made life difficult for Reliance. Singh had overseen a gradual relaxation of the Licence Raj and launched a drive against tax evaders. In March 1986, shortly after Dhirubhai Ambani suffered a stroke, the *Indian Express* published exposes accusing Reliance of smuggling by under-invoicing. There were even rumours of a raid, and Singh was soon shunted out.

Singh had been a nagging thorn in the sensitive Reliance flesh. In May 1985, Singh had removed the import of PTA from the open general licence category. As a raw material, this was crucial for manufacturing polyester filament yarn. This made it very difficult for Reliance Industries to carry on operations; Reliance was able to secure, from various financial institutions, letters of credit that would allow it to import almost one full year's requirement of PTA on the eve of the issuance of the government notification changing the category under which PTA could be imported.

With Singh as Prime Minister, Dhirubhai suffered his first major defeat in the eyes of the public—his futile attempt to take over engineering and construction conglomerate Larsen & Toubro. In 1988, L&T was in a bad shape, and the Ambanis swooped in. Reliance, L&T's biggest private-sector customer, bought a 12.4 per cent of the stake and propelled Mukesh and Anil Ambani on to the L&T board of directors. L&T was awarded a lucrative contract to build Reliance's Hazira petrochemicals plant. There were reports that a state-linked financial company bought L&T shares from India's biggest mutual fund and largest insurance company. It then sold the shares to a small-time investment company connected with Reliance Industries. The L&T chairman soon relinquished his post, and Dhirubhai took over in April 1989.

The *Indian Express* carried out another expose, this time alleging that the takeover had been effected by financial institutions like the Life Insurance Corporation (LIC) and the General Insurance Corporation (GIC) selling their shares. Since these institutions were not legally allowed to sell to private entities, the entire process was seen as fraudulent. Matters went out of hand, and the Ambanis backtracked. An extraordinary general meeting was called to decide whether the Ambanis would remain on the L&T board; Dhirubhai resigned, and the Ambani sons had to flee the venue.

There was another reason, more or less immediate, that possibly made the Ambani family cagey about McDonald's intentions—it had just got the kind of bad press that the Indian media had never dished out to Ambani. In May 1991 (a month before Narasimha Rao would take over as Prime Minister and launch the Liberalisation Era), the *Economist* weekly of the UK carried a survey on India titled 'Caged' with the photograph of a caged tiger on the cover. The author of the survey, Clive Crook, singled out Reliance Industries in his article. Crook[4] contended that the huge Reliance empire epitomised all that was wrong with India—how the country's corporate captains took advantage of favourable regulations to build monopolistic empires. Reliance came across as a corporate entity that had survived and prospered not through someone's keen business acumen, but as a result of political patronage. This upset Dhirubhai Ambani and he reportedly vowed that henceforth the world would look up to Reliance. A foreign reporter (McDonald) with nothing to lose could just well be a loose cannon.

Reliance thereafter put in more effort into media management. By the time Narasimha Rao's Congress-led government was voted out in May 1996, the company had the Indian media firmly in its vice-like grip. There were few news establishments or journalists

---

4   Clive Crook held various editorial positions at the *Economist*, including deputy editor for 11 years. In 2006, he co-chaired the Copenhagen Consensus project, framing global development priorities for the coming decades together with Nobel laureates and other world-renowned economists. He is now a senior editor at the *Atlantic Monthly*.

who spoke or wrote against Reliance. Even the *Indian Express*, the Ambanis' trenchant critic from the mid-1980s, not only threw in the towel, but even went to the extent of supporting the company through its favourable and acquiescent reportage.

Meanwhile, the more McDonald moved around and spoke to people, the more he got sucked in. 'It was the story that no foreign correspondent writes about. They write on the Nehru-Gandhi dynasty, they write on caste wars,' said McDonald. 'When I was thinking of the book, I thought that the political economy of India was something that had not been done since *Mystery of Birla House*.'[5]

The book by Debajyoti Burman, about one of India's most politically influential businessmen, Ghanshyam Das Birla, was published by Jugabani Sahitya Chakra of Calcutta (now Kolkata) in 1950. The book disappeared from the market and was reported to have been sold to the Birlas through a deal possibly in the very late 1950s which eventually included its copyright. Very few copies survived, including one preserved in Delhi's Nehru Memorial Library in the 'rare books' section. McDonald, who had read up enough on Indian business history, saw a parallel here: 'Birla was the golden boy of the Nehruvian years. Dhirubhai was the golden boy of the Indira (Gandhi) and Rajiv (Gandhi) years. Dhirubhai was more or less dictating industrial policy to the government, not just by way of gaining favour, but scuppering his business rivals.' There were to be other parallels too later, albeit differing on hostility levels.

Even as he started getting a 'lot of warnings from people,

---

5   Paranjoy Guha Thakurta was able to procure a copy of this book from Amazon.com, where it was listed under the rare books section. The two-volume *Mystery of Birla House* cost a whopping $220. See annexure: *Mystery of the Birla Book*.

especially fellow journalists, imploring him to be careful,' McDonald 'kept working' but started covering his tracks especially when he was in Mumbai. However, as a result of the freeze in information flow, Dhirubhai Ambani's opponents gradually started opening up to him. They had probably begun to recognise that the writer was not out to do a 'hagiography of Dhirubhai,' that he was not one of Dhirubhai's infamous Dirty Dozen.

This nomenclature was untangled later by McDonald:

Reliance was a pioneer of envelope journalism. A senior commercial journalist in Bombay recalls that journalists would get vouchers worth up to ₹2,000 for goods at a Vimal [a Reliance brand] retail outlet called Laffans. Some in senior positions would get regular monthly payments or issues of Reliance shares and debentures at par. Ambani's moles in the press were known as the 'Dirty Dozen', the journalist said. 'The point man was Rasikbhai Meswani. He was a thorough gentleman. His door was open 24 hours a day for journalists. People would go to collect on first of the month.' Dhirubhai also realised that the reporter was not the final arbiter of what got published.

He also cultivated desk editors and even editors. One who accepted Reliance debentures for himself, and help in arranging bank finance to pay for them, was Girilal Jain, editor of the *Times of India* for much of the 1980s. The close journalists in the 'Dirty Dozen' would not only be used to get favourable news about Reliance printed prominently. They also became an extension of an intelligence network, asking rival businessmen for their frank views off the record about Reliance and then reporting them back. On the theory that rumour and gossip are more keenly heeded because they carry an aura of exclusivity, the pressmen would be used to plant opinions about the merits of Reliance activities and the failings of other companies.

Dhirubhai Ambani certainly had an inkling that McDonald's biography of him would not be a gushing hagiography. The Ambani tycoon, used to having journalists play ball, now faced a man who seemed intent on completing his work and could not be either won or bought over. What is little known is that Reliance Industries reacted even before McDonald could finish the manuscript. In January 1997, he received a letter from Kanga & Co, lawyers for Ambani and Reliance Industries, warning that 'their clients understand and apprehend that the proposed publication contains material which is defamatory to our client.' It was obvious that word had somehow trickled out to Ambani.

The legal letter in a way pre-empted what McDonald was going to write, insisting that at no time had there been any attempt to verify the material with the clients, and action for exemplary damages and injunction would be made if the book was defamatory. The veiled threat did not deter McDonald; he carried on undaunted and unrattled. The pre-emptive strike did not work.

Reliance Industries was unwilling to give up lightly. Its lawyers in Sydney—Blake Dawson (now known as Ashurst Australia)—sent legal notices to McDonald's Australian publisher Allen and Unwin warning of punitive action if their clients were defamed. The notices quoted passages verbatim from the HarperCollins India version in support of their contention that the author was aiming to defame Dhirubhai Ambani.

The chief executive officer of Allen and Unwin, Patrick Gallagher, did not cower down either. Once the manuscript had been completed, he had a Sydney barrister go through it meticulously. Changes were suggested and the author was asked for material to back up facts. Towards the end of 1997, Allen and Unwin moved ahead with an initial print run of 3,000. The detailed chronicle was at long last published in early 1998, and titled *The Polyester Prince: The Rise of Dhirubhai Ambani*.

The Indian edition ran into trouble. HarperCollins India, which had the Indian rights, had completed editing the manuscript and even started having pages printed, though those had not been collated and bound as a book. The tittle-tattle that made their way to McDonald and his publisher in Australia was that Reliance was seeking injunctions against the book's publication at the high courts in Ahmedabad and Delhi.

'The interesting thing was that in the papers sent to us were passages from the book which at that stage had not been published. Reliance claimed that the pages had been sent to them by 'a well-wisher,' recollected McDonald. Towards end-1998, the company moved the lower district court of Tis Hazari in Delhi, and procured an injunction against publication. It was a temporary injunction that was never vacated (a temporary injunction restrains publication for a specific period of time).

And then, the much-awaited book simply disappeared from the Indian landscape. Even ahead of the injunction, HarperCollins had pulped its edition; and the Australian publisher refrained from selling into India's jurisdiction. McDonald could never have guessed that his work would effectively meet the same fate as the book that he had admiringly talked about: *Mystery of Birla House*. Rumours abounded and conspiracy theories wafted through corridors of power and in press clubs. Where did the copies disappear?

Towards the end of 1998, during a chance meeting with HarperCollins editor Renuka Chatterjee at the Frankfurt Book Fair, McDonald came to know of the reason for pulping the book. HarperCollins had received legal threats as well as notices of pre-publication injunctions warning that Reliance Industries would launch applications for injunction at every high court in India, and with twenty-two of them, the publisher was distraught about having to spend a fortune defending the book. Cases like these drag on for years, and the book would never be published. Chatterjee also received calls dissuading her from going ahead with the publication, though she was not physically threatened. HarperCollins decided not to proceed with the publication and all printed-but-unbound copies were pulped.

When injunction notices reached Allen and Unwin in Sydney, the publisher sent back a note saying they were not publishing the book in India, that it was confined to Australia, and therefore Indian courts had no jurisdiction over their actions. Allen and Unwin said that it would not attend the court hearing, and never got a copy of the ruling. McDonald recalled that journalist friends who went down to the court to obtain information for a story returned empty-handed.

The book disappeared, but the story didn't—it kept developing. In July 2002, Dhirubhai Ambani died intestate—without leaving a will. The sons, Mukesh and Anil, remained united for two years after Ambani's death. But the undercurrents of tension between the siblings were known only to company insiders till November 2004 when Mukesh Ambani publicly acknowledged that there were 'ownership issues' between him and Anil. Then on, till July 2005, the two brothers fought a bitter, no-holds barred battle in the public. Allegations and counter-allegations flew thick and fast, till a ceasefire was brokered by their mother Kokilaben and leading banker KV Kamath, ex-head of ICICI (formerly Industrial Credit & Investment Corporation of India) Bank. The truce lasted for three years.

In January 2008, almost ten years after it was effectively banned in India (technically it was never banned since it had never been published), photocopied versions of *The Polyester Prince* mysteriously appeared on the crowded pavements and at busy traffic signals in Mumbai. Pirated copies were sold at varying prices—from a measly ₹100 to an exorbitant ₹1,600. The timing of the curious incident raised eyebrows, since copies of the book had landed with street vendors and hawkers on 13 and 14 January, just two days before the IPO (initial public offering) of Anil Ambani's Reliance Power Ltd opened for subscription. Very curious, indeed. Both Mukesh Ambani's Reliance Industries Limited (RIL) and his younger brother's Anil Dhirubhai Ambani Group (ADAG) declined to comment on the pirated book that sold like hot cakes.

This also came in the backdrop of the blockbuster film *Guru*, said to have been loosely strung around the life and times of Dhirubhai Ambani. The 2007 biopic, written and directed by Mani Ratnam, had ostensibly drawn substantial 'inspiration' from McDonald's chronicle. That, of course, was a mix of speculation and hearsay. Ratnam described *Guru* as having been inspired by stories both past and present, but the cheeky allusions were clear and unmistakable. There were hawkers in Mumbai who peddled the book as being the source material for the film. McDonald recalled being gravely disappointed at the time. 'Let a book be published and then be sued,' he told an Indian newspaper at the time. 'It getting blocked even before it can hit the stands is a serious infringement on the right to free speech.' And then he thought aloud, and gave an inkling of either an update or a sequel: 'I have been keeping up-to-date with the actions of the two brothers and am thinking of an update. I wish I find a publisher who is brave enough to publish the book in India.'

All this time, McDonald stayed abreast of the Ambani goings-on, and meanwhile worked on other projects. In July 2000, he and Desmond Ball, a professor at the Australian National University and world-renowned expert on intelligence matters, published *Death in Balibo, Lies in Canberra* that was an incriminating documentation of the criminal connivance of the Australian government in the deaths of five journalists in Balibo, East Timor. The meticulously-researched and riveting study had revealed the workings of a clandestine system of deceit, and named those involved in a 24-year trail of flagrant cover-ups and abject denials. McDonald and Ball explored how, at first light on 16 October 1975, Indonesian special forces stormed the East Timor village of Balibo, killing the five reporters.

Between 1997 and 2000, as foreign editor with the *Sydney Morning Herald*, he covered the Asian financial crisis, the collapse of the Suharto regime, and the East Timor crisis. In 2002, McDonald moved on to Beijing, and in 2005 won the Walkley Award for newspaper feature writing for his article *What's Wrong With Falun Gong*, a story about the brutal suppression of the Falun Gong religious movement by the Chinese government.

All the while earlier that McDonald had been researching and writing *The Polyester Prince*, he was told more than once that the Ambani family was itself working on a volume on the life and times of Dhirubhai Ambani. The family indeed was, and the effort saw the light of day in the form of a voluminous, slickly-produced opus titled *Dhirubhai Ambani: The Man I Knew*, published in March 2007 under the name of his widow Kokilaben. The bulky, 300+ paged product (the Gujarati edition was titled *Dhirubhai Ambani: Maara Jeevan Sathi*) was a coffee-table book, one that was conceptualised and supervised by Dipti Salgaocar, Dhirubhai's elder daughter. It was described as Kokilaben's own effort to 'present him as a man who was much more than the person the world saw.' It was personal, colourful.

Later in the year, another book was released, this one by an old associate of Dhirubhai Ambani—AG Krishnamurthy, founder of advertising agency Mudra Communications. When Krishnamurthy started Mudra in March 1980, he had only one client: Reliance. The agency's first major campaign was the launch of Reliance's apparel and textiles brand Vimal with the catchy tagline 'Only Vimal'. Mudra was later acquired by the Omnicom Group in 2011, subsequently rebranded as DDB Mudra group, and merged with DDB Worldwide. But Krishnamurthy's association with Ambani had withstood the onslaught of time.

His *Dhirubhaism—The Remarkable Work Philosophy of Dhirubhai Ambani* was published by McGraw Hill Education in April 2007. It was that typical hands-on book for budding entrepreneurs and managers. Krishnamurthy followed this up with another title in less than a year: *Dhirubhai Ambani—Against All Odds: A Story of Courage, Perseverance and Hope*. The Ambani patriarch was long gone, but public interest in him hadn't faded away; he remained an inspiration for budding entrepreneurs.

And just as McDonald kept returning to Indonesia (he had co-authored another book on that country in the interregnum: *Masters of Terror: Indonesia's Military & Violence in East Timor*, 1999), India too kept beckoning him through the never-ending Ambani saga, that kept him fascinated with its innumerable twists, unseemly turns and intriguing plots. Soon, he got cracking on an updated version of *The Polyester Prince*. 'India was now the new darling of the business world. So I said, well, here is a chance to actually make some money; so I added a few more chapters,' said McDonald.

In 2010, an updated but sanitised version of *The Polyester Prince* was published by NewSouth Publishing as *Mahabharata in Polyester: The Making of the World's Richest Brothers and Their Feud*. The Indian edition was published by Roli Books, New Delhi— albeit with a different title, *Ambani & Sons*. It was later learnt that

the head of Roli Books, Pramod Kapur had met an important
functionary of the Anil Dhirubhai Ambani Group (ADAG) before
the title was published. The functionary reportedly told Kapur
that he need not worry too much about the legal consequences of
publishing *Ambani & Sons* as, by then, the open battle between the
Ambani siblings had attracted considerable media attention. Still,
the detailed introduction from the original work where McDonald
had delineated his encounter with Dhirubhai down to the pre-
publication injunction against the book was left out.

Passing mention of an alleged attack on Tina Munim, whose
wedding with Anil that the writer had attended, was expunged,
as was another passing remark about a murderous attempt on
the life of Nusli Wadia. The English explanation of Chorwad as a
'settlement of thieves' was inked out, though the original book had
clearly said 'though no one seems to remark on that.'

References to the Gandhi family and others like then finance
minister and later President of India, Pranab Mukherjee, were
either toned down or removed altogether. A so-called 'parting gift'
by Prime Minister Indira Gandhi before the general elections of
1977 which she lost, found no mention.

> In March 1977, however, Indira and Congress were swept
> from power in the elections called after her two years' rule
> under Emergency powers was lifted. But her government gave
> Dhirubhai a parting gift. Over the 1976–77 fiscal year (April-
> March) Dhirubhai had accumulated REP licences[6] both from its
> own exports and from purchases in the market, worth some ₹3
> crore. On 7 February, about three weeks after the elections were
> announced; the government was persuaded to exempt all polyester

---

6   REP, or replenished licences were granted to exporters enabling them to
    import goods at a time when India was going through a shortage of foreign
    currency.

yarn imports under REP licences issued since April 1976 from customs duty, which was then 125 per cent. It was a gift of ₹3.75 crore to Dhirubhai.

This fiscal move had been allegedly facilitated by Mukherjee, a great friend of Dhirubhai. McDonald said Roli Books primarily wanted the references to Pranab Mukherjee to be slashed out. 'Pranab was back as minister for finance in Manmohan Singh's government and Roli (Books) was pretty worried that he still had the power to turn the inspectors on Roli's books,' contended McDonald, later a fellow at the American think-tank Woodrow Wilson Centre.

Other references to Mukherjee too were truncated, robbing the new book of the compelling context:

> As well as an always-open connection to the prime minister's office, he now had a close and sympathetic friend as minister of commerce, the Bengali politician Pranab Mukherjee. His ministry not only helped set trade policy, including tariff levels and anti-dumping duties, in conjunction with the ministry of finance, but conducted the system of import licences through the powerful office of the chief controller of imports and exports—whose corridors in New Delhi's Udyog Bhavan were thronged with importunate businessmen and their agents.

> At the beginning of 1982 Mukherjee became minister of finance, giving him charge of broad economic policy as well as the details of revenue raising and tax enforcement. The ministry of finance also supervised the Reserve Bank of India, the central bank, whose governor is often a recently retired head of the ministry. Through its banking division the ministry also effectively directed the 26 nationalised banks through highly politicised board and senior management appointments. It supervised the insurance companies and other financial institutions such as the Unit Trust

of India, and controlled entry to the sharemarkets by Indian companies.

In another instance,

> Editorials asked how closely the central bank had scrutinised the eligibility of the 11 companies under the NRI [non-resident Indian] scheme, if the finance minister could not even get their domicile right. 'Pranab Mukherjee: Minister of Finance or Reliance?' went the headline in the *Telegraph's* leader. Facing more questions in parliament and an attempted breach of privilege motion (rejected by the Congress majority) on 14 December (1983), Mukherjee insisted the different place of incorporation 'did not make any material difference' about eligibility and appealed to MPs not to 'kill the scheme.'

simply became:

> Editorials asked how closely the central bank had scrutinised the eligibility of the 11 companies under the NRI scheme, if the finance minister could not even get their domicile right. On 14 December, Mukherjee insisted the different place of incorporation 'did not make any material difference' about eligibility and appealed to MPs not to 'kill the scheme.'

In 1984, Reliance was given letters of intent for a 75,000 tonne a year purified terephthalic acid (PTA) plant at Patalganga in Maharashtra. The *fait accompli* of its 25,125 tonne polyester filament yarn plant was retrospectively endorsed by raising the permitted capacity from the original 12,000 tonnes. *Sunday* magazine reported the granting of this largesse under the tell-tale headline 'Pranab Mukherjee's Slogan: Only Vimal.' The mention of the headline was left out of *Ambani & Sons*.

Thus, many could argue that the book was more of an indictment of the moth-eaten Indian fiscal system than of Ambani himself.

The *New York Times* review (almost a year later) felt 'McDonald is respectful of Ambani's remarkable trail of innovation and success,' and went on to remark:

> Much of the criticism of Ambani is, in effect, of the Indian system of bureaucratic controls, state intervention, high but variable tariffs, industrial and import licensing, state control of unit trusts and life insurance. To beat the system to get ahead, it was necessary to exploit the human frailties of its power holders. Everyone did it. Ambani did it most effectively.

Some of these, mentioned in the context of bureaucrat Nitish Sengupta, were dropped as well:

> In 1969, Sengupta had helped in the abolition of the managing agency's system, whereby families such as the Tatas wielded control over affiliated companies with very little equity, and in preparing the Monopolies and Restrictive Trade Practices Act 1969 which intensified the industrial licensing regime first introduced in 1951. Other measures which followed included the 'convertibility clause,' whereby the government financial institutions (development banks providing long-term finance and insurance companies) were given the option to convert a proportion of long-term loans to companies into equity, and the Foreign Exchange Regulation Act 1973 which sharply restricted the freedom of Indians to hold foreign currency or assets.

> On his arrival at the Ministry of Finance in 1979, Sengupta had already begun the transition in thinking that led him to write in his 1995 memoir, *Inside the Steel Frame*:

>> The possession of vast unregulated power in the hands of the ministers and the bureaucrats inevitably led to complaints of extortion, inducement and enormous politicisation of the machinery. From 1970 supreme power was appropriated by

the cabinet committee on economic co-ordination which was headed by the prime minister and for all practical purposes the prime minister's office became the main decision-making authority. No worthwhile project could be cleared without the prime minister's approval. Those who managed to get industrial licences also managed to see to it that others did not. This was done by money, influence and political muscle power. A nexus came to be established between a section of industrialists, a section of politicians and a section of bureaucrats. The principle of market forces guiding or dictating investment, or of production targets being determined by demand and supply, was given the go-by, and everything was decided by administrative fiat.

There was more: the virtual extortion of Nusli Wadia by Congress scion Sanjay Gandhi, with tacit approval of his mother Indira, who had just stormed back to power in January 1980.

> Wadia was directed first to meet Sanjay Gandhi, who made a blunt demand for a political donation. Wadia demurred. ~~"Sorry, we just don't do that,' he said. 'None of us - the Tatas, the Mahindras, us give money to political parties. We do not have black income. It's just not something we do.'~~ On being shown in to Mrs Indira Gandhi, and having presented the company history, Wadia ~~broke the subject directly. He knew the reason he had been summoned, but really it was not the way his company operated. He talked on, and then~~ noticed Indira was doodling on papers on her desk, looking away. Wadia took his leave, and received a curt nod from Indira Gandhi.[7]

If there were real villains who actually subverted the system, they were Congress politicians. So, few could disagree with the

---

7   The struck out instances were removed in the modified version.

contention (that came through the book, according to the NYT review) that 'Ambani would have been a hugely successful businessman anywhere.' McDonald had written a classic tale of why business and politics should not mix. Therefore, had the Ambani sons over-reacted to the book?

Historian Ramachandra Guha, writing in the *Telegraph* newspaper about book bans in India much later (in July 2011), explained that 'the descendants or devotees of biographical subjects are often too nervous or insecure to have them discussed with objectivity and rigour. Second, these fanatical or insecure followers have found an ally in the courts. Although the Supreme Court has tended to act on the side of the freedom of expression, lower courts have been less wise. Judges who are malleable or publicity-hungry pass injunctions forbidding the free circulation of books and works of art. Few petitioners have the time, or money, or energy, to wait and fight till the case reaches the Supreme Court (a process that can take years). A ban once invoked is therefore rarely revoked.'

McDonald was to write in *Outlook* magazine much later in March 2014, 'In the case of my book *The Polyester Prince*, about the Reliance patriarch Dhirubhai Ambani, my main surprise was that HarperCollins India, under Renuka Chatterjee, had the chutzpah to even attempt to publish. Threats to seek injunctions in every high court across India, and some heavy phone calls, got the edition pulped. The injunction, obtained without contest from a junior beak in the Tis Hazari court house, was a superfluous *coup de grace*. Ambani's sons had the grace not to attempt the same with Roli Books' updated version, *Ambani & Sons*, and let it stand or fall on its merits.' McDonald's observations came in a feature section where six authors wrote about their books being banned in India.

All said and done, *Ambani & Sons*, however, never became a talking point as its earlier avatar. In 2010 and even now, if a book is bandied around as one that should be read and discussed, it is *The Polyester Prince*. There are many reasons why this remains a classic case study.

First, the book came to be pulped even before it had been published. There is a perceptible difference between something that 'is defamatory' and something that 'might be defamatory.' Unless an entire body of work or an extract or even an insinuation has been proven to be defamatory, it is only a conjecture. In that, the injunction set a deadly precedent. This was not about a book being banned; it was about a book being stopped from being published altogether.

Second, the publisher buckled under pressure over threats, and not an actual legal action (except for the Delhi injunction). HarperCollins was allegedly threatened with multiple injunctions. The very prospect of such a scenario, wherein it would have to fight out a legal battle in a number of courts, made it drop the manuscript like hot coals—it was not willing to fight for free speech. There have been innumerable instances when publishers, soft targets themselves, have caved in to threats or pressures, leaving their writers to fight lonely battles. These Indian publishers come across as duplicitous when they even talk of free expression—track records show that they are often the first to flee the battlefield.

Third, the disappearance of the book raised questions on whether India had grown mature enough to browse through unapologetic and unflattering accounts of captains of industry who the Indian public held in high esteem and even revered. It was clear that a corporate entity could arm-twist a publishing house from publishing an incisive and investigative narrative about its alleged misdoings.

Fourth, while neither the (Indian) publisher nor the writer could make any money from sales, the action of Reliance Industries did have its Streisand Effect.[8] Though a handful of copies did find their way into India initially, the fact that pirated copies sold like hot cakes even ten years after the virtual ban, showed that people were curious, that they hadn't forgotten the book all this while, and that people certainly wanted to know what was it that the Ambanis did not want the citizenry to know. Worse, it conjured up an image of the Ambanis that they might not have wanted in the first place: that of a sinister corporation that not only flouted laws, but also did everything to suppress that information.

Fifth, McDonald's work was of exemplary journalistic value. Here was a reporter who wasn't a son of the soil, but had both the percipience and drive of a hard-boiled reporter: he dug out dirt and pieced things together. McDonald's was the classic journalism style: follow the evidence, and go wherever it leads you. His tenacity and copybook style of investigative journalism would go on to inspire and provoke others to work on long-form, narrative pieces of journalistic work.

Yet, non-action by the Ambani brothers against *Ambani & Sons* was seen by many as the maturing of the two; that they had learnt

---

8   The Streisand Effect, as defined in Wikipedia, is the phenomenon whereby an attempt to hide, remove or censor a piece of information has the unintended consequence of publicising the information more widely. It is named after American entertainer Barbra Streisand, whose May 2003 attempt to suppress aerial photographs of her residence in Malibu, California inadvertently drew sizeable public attention to it. The term was coined by Mike Masnick of Techdirt in 2005, after Streisand unsuccessfully sued photographer Kenneth Adelman and Pictopia.com for violation of privacy for $50 million. Before Streisand filed her lawsuit, the image had been downloaded from Adelman's website only six times; twice by Streisand's own attorneys. After the lawsuit, more than 420,000 people visited the site over the following month.

to live with the times, and also live with the irrefutable fact that not all reportage and opinions need necessarily be in your favour. Their individual reactions to *Gas Wars* probably told a different story; but then, neither had let the push come to a shove.

2

A Story, Told Finally

The late 1990s—when journalist Hamish McDonald was working feverishly towards wrapping up his book about Dhirubhai Ambani and his Reliance Industries Limited (RIL)—were exciting times for both business and business journalism. The seeds of liberalisation, sown by the Rajiv Gandhi dispensation and nurtured two Prime Ministers later by the PV Narasimha Rao regime, were beginning to yield fruits. Business was no longer just a particular reporter's beat, the pink papers were flourishing, business-to-business (B2B) publications were beginning to take roots, and business journalists now had the luxury of delving deep beyond the mundane headlines and straightjacket stories.

More money matters meant banks and banking regulations would come increasingly under scrutiny of the public in general and journalists in particular, and more would be written about both financial irregularities as well as loopholes in the regulatory mechanism. The Reserve Bank of India (RBI) itself was aware of the faultlines in its system, and started reining in those who were operating virtually outside its purview: mostly residuary non-banking companies, or RNBCs for short.[9] By this time the RBI had already been able to assert some control over the Peerless Group, the largest shadow-banking organisation of the time, after spending years in legal wrangles with it. In January 1996, the Supreme Court agreed, while issuing a judgment, that companies like Peerless indeed had a role to play in an economy where small savings were not tapped by big commercial banks, and in the same breath emphasised the RBI's authority to monitor and supervise such companies, and enforce regulatory provisions.

Growing at an accelerating pace at this time was the Sahara India Pariwar. Everything about the organisation and the man who ran it, Subrata Roy, was larger than life. Yet, little was known about either. There would be bizarre rumours about how surreal the working atmosphere in the organisation was, and there would be unsubstantiated and unverifiable accounts about how Sahara was raking in its millions. In November 1994, the Sahara India Savings & Investment Corporation Limited, a Sahara company, rechristened itself as Sahara India Financial Corporation Limited (SIFCL) after being in existence for seven years, and four years later was given a RNBC registration by the RBI. The increasing pace of growth of the company then became frenetic—it would have a deposit portfolio of ₹20,000 crore by July 2008 when it made public its unaudited financial results for the first time.

If Dhirubhai Ambani and his RIL had an alleged reputation: that of bending the rules or having regulations devised specifically for them; Subrata Roy was said to operate either outside the

---

9   A residuary non-banking company (RNBC) is a special type of a non-banking finance company (NBFC) which has as its principal business the receiving of deposits, under any scheme or arrangement or any other manner, and not being an investment, asset financing, loan-advancing company. These companies are now required to maintain investments as per directions of the Reserve Bank of India, in addition to liquid assets.

realm of the RBI's jurisdiction, or make a mockery of the loopholes in the capital market system. Watching all this from the sidelines was Tamal Bandopadhyay, who had started out as a trainee journalist with the *Times of India* in Mumbai, and then worked with the *Economic Times*, *Financial Express* and *Business Standard*. As a business journalist specialising in banking and finance, Bandopadhyay kept a close watch on Sahara India Pariwar and remained engrossed with it. 'I remember around 2005 or a few years later when Sahara was fighting it out with the banking regulator (the RBI), I was following it very closely. Those days, it was not easy to get hold of the annual reports of unlisted companies as the Registrar of Companies did not have the kind of website where one could pay a token fee and access annual reports (which we do now). It was very difficult to access those reports, and I really had to work hard to procure them from Lucknow. They were all a goldmine of information,' he told the authors of this book.

The very subject of RNBCs too fascinated him. 'I always wondered why they were called 'residuary' and did not have the answer till DN Ghosh told me: for want of a specific name, a finance ministry bureaucrat one late evening named these companies so. He was in a hurry as the file had to be cleared that night. Its business model—it could take deposits but could not lend—was interesting. When you are allowed to take deposits but cannot lend, how do you make money? I wanted to find an answer to this.' Ghosh was a former finance ministry official who took over as Peerless's managing director in August 1996 long after having retired as chairman of the public sector State Bank of India (SBI) in 1989.

RNBCs, particularly Peerless and Sahara, were to be the RBI's prime targets once Yaga Venugopal Reddy took over as its

governor in September 2003. His five-year term, in the words of
Bandopadhyay, 'was characterised by the highest average growth
rate achieved by the Indian economy and the lowest average
inflation since Independence.' Reddy was clear about the two
RNBC giants; he wanted to close them down. 'His objective was
to protect depositors' interests at any cost and he did that without
caring about the power and influence wielded by the RNBCs.' When
the real confrontation between the Sahara India Pariwar and the
RBI happened, Bandopadhyay had moved on to *Mint* as part of its
founding team. He still observed the developments, most of which
happened in the last six months of Reddy's tenure. The drama
began with the RBI asking Sahara to reduce its deposit liability,[10]
and culminated in Sahara agreeing to reconstitute the SIFCL board
of directors. RBI reined in Sahara through manoeuvres outlined in
detail by Bandopadhyay.

The other regulator that Sahara had to encounter—the Securities
and Exchange Board of India (SEBI)—however had a trying time in
controlling Subrata Roy's group. The confrontation began after SEBI
in December 2009 received a complaint from one Professional
Group for Investor Protection alleging that the Sahara India Real
Estate Corporation Limited (SIRECL) had been issuing optionally
fully convertible debentures, or OFCDs for short,[11] to investors for
months, and this it was doing without disclosing so in the draft
prospectus. The battle trundled on from the Securities Appellate
Tribunal (SAT) to the Lucknow bench of the Allahabad High Court
to the Supreme Court. Roy kept cocking a snook at SEBI.

---

10 Deposit liabilities (or liability) is the money that people and companies
    have put into banks, and that the banks would have to pay back at some
    time in the future.
11 An optionally fully convertible debenture (OFCD) is a type of debt security
    where the option is given to the holder if he/she wants to convert the
    debenture into equity share after a stipulated time.

Even as Bandopadhyay kept an eye on the Sahara-SEBI developments, he pursued his interest in banks and banking matters and completed a book on HDFC Bank. Charting the growth of India's largest private bank in terms of market capitalisation was not difficult—it was among the first private banks to be established after the RBI issued new licenses in 1994, and had grown phenomenally all through Bandopadhyay's journalistic career. *A Bank for the Buck*, published in November 2012, told through an anecdote-filled narrative the extraordinary story of a 'steady, boring and monotonous bank.' He spoke to commercial bankers, investment bankers, regulators, central bankers, economists, corporate borrowers and investors in the bank; he steered clear of economic data and strung together a saga that would interest ordinary readers. All that Bandopadhyay, a student of English literature, had done was narrate a story.

The story did not run afoul of anyone. Bereft of banking jargon and devoid of numbers, it came as a refreshing change in the publishing history of Indian financial institutions. There were not too many controversies to deal with any way. The first time HDFC Bank landed in a big spot was, in fact, a few months after the publication of Bandopadhyay's book, when investigative portal Cobrapost in March 2013 released video footage from its 'Operation Red Spider' showing high-ranking officials and some employees of HDFC Bank and two other banks, willing to turn black money into white. Investigations by the RBI could not find any *prima facie* violation of the Prevention of Money Laundering Act, 2002 but there were other transgressions—that of KYC (know your customer) norms.[12] HDFC Bank was fined ₹4.5 crore.

---

12 Know your customer (KYC) is the process of a business verifying the identity of its clients. The term is also used to refer to the bank regulations which governs these activities.

The day after *A Bank for the Buck* was released, on 30
November a desperate Sahara went knocking at the doors of the
Supreme Court, pleading for more time to refund its investors.
The apex court had already upheld a SAT directive ordering
refund of ₹24,029 crore to 29.6 million investors. Sahara had
been pushed into a corner finally, and it was possibly time for
writing a book on the group. Bandopadhyay, who had been toying
with the idea for a while, now decided to go the whole hog. In
January 2013, he landed at Sahara Shaher—the township that's
home to the group on the banks of the Gomti river in Lucknow—
to interview Subrata Roy, and even attended Roy's extravagant
39th wedding anniversary celebrations. The interview itself was
exhaustive, candid. 'From there, the project took off. I planned it
well and could complete it in about six months' intense work and
extensive travel across India. Of course, I could complete it in a
relatively short time as I was extremely familiar with the subject,'
recalled Bandopadhyay.

The subject of Sahara needed a large canvas—as that of a book,
rather than a series of articles on the company and its doings and
alleged misdoings. Bandopadhyay explained, 'As a journalist, for
about a decade, I had been following Sahara India Pariwar which
had 4,799 establishments and businesses under 16 verticals and
claimed to be the second largest employer in the country after the
Indian Railways. Only four companies in the group had been listed
(at least one of them got delisted later). India's largest shadow
bank in the form of a RNBC was under the Sahara fold till the
RBI forced its closure.

'The glitz and glamour associated with the group boss
Subrata Roy and the mystery that shrouded its business always
fascinated me as a journalist. I was curious to know how Roy
arbitraged between Bharat and India—the two nations, one full

of poverty and other glamour, cricket, Bollywood, patriotism. People in Bharat looked at him in awe because of his proximity to cricketers and filmstars. That's how he built trust. It was a fascinating story.' This was the story that Bandopadhyay wanted to tell his readers.

The book on Sahara was to be an attempt at unraveling the mystery. 'I had written quite a few long-form pieces in *Mint* and in my earlier paper, *Business Standard*, but if you want to create an impact, a book is always a better vehicle. Also, a typical Indian newspaper cannot probably afford the time and resources one requires to research such kind of subjects. I travelled extensively across India to meet people who had been associated with the group in some form and other, besides regulators and courts in different Indian states to get hold of documents. Affidavits and petitions filed in courts are always an authentic source of information,' the journalist recollected.

That Bandopadhyay was working on a book on Sahara and Subrata Roy was no secret. Sometime in October–November 2013, he was invited to talk about the book at a literary festival at the India Habitat Centre in New Delhi. Though the book was not yet ready, the *Business Today* editor, who was present at the festival, asked for a chapter which the magazine could publish. They were handed over one.

It is not clear whether after reading the chapter that the Sahara group asked for a copy of the yet-to-be-published book, or the publisher volunteered to send a copy of the book to Sahara for eye-balling before its formal release. The fact remained that the group got hold of a copy of the manuscript and rushed to slap a ₹200 crore defamation suit against the author and publisher at Calcutta High Court. On 10 December 2013, the high court granted the group's plea for a stay on the release of *Sahara: The Untold Story*, and the court extended that interim order on 23 December until further orders. The group also made Jaico Publishing House, the publisher of the book, a party to the suit.

It was a classic case of pleading for prior restraint along the lines of the action against *The Polyester Prince*. In its 10 December order, the single-judge bench referred to one passage that had been cited by Sahara's counsel:

> More such incredible tales abound about Sahara, none that could be substantiated. A group employee in Mumbai asked me whether I had seen the 'torture chamber' in Sahara Shaher. What's that, I asked. The chamber, apparently, is where an erring employee is dumped at night in his underwear and subjected to physical abuse and humiliations by his subordinates, including his driver and guards if he's of high office. Sahara does this to shame a rogue employee and destroy his self-respect and dignity, the group employee said. A communication executive at Sahara laughed when I checked with him about the authenticity of the torture chamber.

The judge went on to rule:

> *Prima facie*, the impugned materials do show the plaintiffs in poor light. Since the book or any electronic form of the material has not been published as yet, the balance of convenience lies in restraining its publication till the *prima facie* case is more fully brought out in the presence of the defendants.

Bandopadhyay never received the notice himself as it was served at the office of HT Media (which owned *Mint*) in Kolkata. 'It was on 12 December 2013 that my publisher Jaico told me about the development. I met a nervous Akash (Shah), my publisher, that evening at a hotel in Lower Parel, Mumbai. I persuaded him not to back out and fight it out in court as I could support with documentary evidence every word of the book. Quite a few law firms in Mumbai and Kolkata were willing to fight for me in the courts. I chose Fox & Mondal which worked for me *pro bono*. Akash employed a separate law firm.'

'At the very first hearing at a trial court before the Christmas vacation, the judge told my lawyer to put in ₹200 crore in an escrow account if we wanted to go ahead with the publication of the book. Those were tough days. I did not have to spend anything as legal expenses but had to rush to Kolkata frequently to meet my law firm and prepare my lawyer for the case. *Mint* stood by me, freeing me from my daily chores in office. My wife and son were pillars of support.' Beyond the trial court, Bandopadhyay moved a two-judge divisional bench of Calcutta High Court at the advice of his law firm and also started planning to subsequently move the Supreme Court with a special leave petition (SLP).

The aggression that Sahara showed in the case of the book belied the face-saving brave front that it was frantically trying to put on in the Supreme Court, which had in November 2013 placed restrictions on the group's sale of moveable and immoveable property and also barred Roy from leaving the country. In January 2014, the apex court directed the Sahara Group to reveal the source of the ₹22,885 crore that had been paid to OFCD investors. It warned Sahara of inquiries by the Central Bureau of Investigation (CBI) and the Registrar of Companies if it failed to reveal the source.

'As the media—both international and in India—started extensively reporting on my case, the group probably thought it was not wise to fight on so many fronts. A feeler was sent to me for discussion. I agreed to discuss and move ahead. We had rounds of discussion at Sahara Star Hotel near the domestic airport in Mumbai. The meetings lasted for long hours, at times from afternoon till early morning of the next day. Since I was not willing to drop things from the book that the group wanted me to do, a compromise was reached whereby the publisher would carry the disclaimer which says the book is 'defamatory' and also offered the group's point of view,' Bandopadhyay said.

But since Sahara had a history of dragging everyone to court—from the RBI to SEBI, surely Bandopadhyay expected them to confront him the same legal way? 'Not really. I was not prepared for legal action, even though my publisher was very apprehensive. The publisher consulted a legal firm, got the manuscript read over and over again, and asked me many questions to check whether I could stand by what I had written and whether those would hold good in a court of law. Following the queries by legal experts, I tweaked the manuscript wherever it was needed and kept all documentary evidence in my possession to support my thesis,' he responded.

In any case, the project was not guerrilla warfare, i.e. journalistic assault by stealth. 'I took Roy and his group in confidence right from the beginning. I had spent two days with him in January 2013 in Sahara Shaher, Lucknow, and played back an hour-long interview. Roy's office got back to me with clarifications which I accommodated. I also accessed some photographs from the group's archive. All were done transparently with an explicit understanding that I was working on a book project besides a long form story for *Mint*. However, I never showed the manuscript (to Roy/Sahara). To be fair to the group, it did not ask for it either. Probably, Roy expected something else and my treatment disappointed him.'

The negotiations could have well reminded Bandopadhyay of the many parleys that he had himself reconstructed in his book. One of the most riveting was the fast-paced account about the two meetings with RBI officials that eventually brought the Sahara

India Pariwar down on to its knees. Apart from the description of the roller-coaster ride that had happened behind the scenes, what also came out from the story was how formidable the Sahara folks were—they were no meek pushovers. The RBI team, represented by its toughest members, had to use every cell in their brains to hem in the Sahara officials.

And here was Bandopadhyay battling the same firm and its unyielding squad of negotiators on his own. 'Indeed there was pressure on me to drop many references, change things, etc, but I would not call it (the negotiations) hostile. The meetings were long, and out of sheer fatigue one could have agreed to things which they were suggesting. An external communications agency was doing the mediation. Sahara was represented by its communications division, backed by the legal cell. There was nobody present from the legal cell at the meetings, but it was consulted extensively over phone. I was alone at the discussion table. There was a steady flow of food, soft drinks and we even had beer in the evening once.'

Bandopadhyay also met Roy twice at his Mumbai office—once before the negotiations started, and another time when they were close to reaching an agreement. On the second occasion, he hosted dinner for the writer. 'He was polite and nice to me; there was no hostility.'

Other developments were taking place parallelly. When the Sahara India Pariwar had taken on the RBI and SEBI, it had continuously thumbed its nose at the two regulators and seemed undaunted by their legal/constitutional status. It would issue rhetorical full-paged advertisements in newspapers and carry on with its business as usual. Roy and his group met their eventual Waterloo when they carried on with their irreverence a bit too far—with the Supreme Court. On 20 February 2014, the court ordered Roy to be personally present in court six days later over the failure of his group companies to return money to the holders of OFCDs. Roy did not appear, citing his mother's illness, prompting the court to issue a non-bailable warrant.

What the court said on 26 February 2014 was significant. Dismissing the counsel's request for excusing Roy from personally appearing before the court in view of his mother's illness, the bench of justices KS Radhakrishnan and JS Khehar remarked, 'Since, we have already declined to grant exemption from personal presence of alleged contemnor no. 5 (Roy) on 25 February, we find no reason to accede to the renewal of the request made today.' The judges also noted that the medical certificate produced as evidence to show his mother's health condition was issued, of all institutions, by the Sahara Hospital in Lucknow. 'In our view, the factual position indicated therein does not solicit the exemption sought. The arms of this court are very long. We will get him here if he does not want to come on his own. If other directors can come, why can't he? Yesterday only we had refused your plea for exemption from personal appearance. All this is going on for last two years. We are issuing non-bailable warrant now,' the judges said.

Roy was arrested in Lucknow two days later after he surrendered to the police, and was kept in police custody. The Supreme Court on 4 March sent Roy and other directors of the Sahara India Pariwar to Tihar jail after he failed to convince the judges about his proposals to refund investors. [At the time of this book going to the press, Roy was still in jail.] In April 2014, Sahara withdrew its defamation suit against Bandopadhyay and Jaico after, what was described as, 'an amicable settlement.'

The book was released in May 2014, and carried both on the back cover and the front-inside flap, apart from an insertion that preceded the dedication page, a statement from the Sahara India Pariwar.

The disclaimer went:

The book *Sahara: The Untold Story*, written by Shri Tamal Bandopadhyay, is based on a particular notion, wrong perceptions supported by limited and skewed information. Hence, it does not reflect the true and complete picture.

The book portrays Sahara in bad light by attributing unfound facts and incidents to which we have objections.

The book also overlooks, or at the best just glances over, the contributions made by Sahara India Pariwar by financially including the poor and rural India, and inculcating in them the habit of saving, thus paving the road of progress on the one hand and safeguarding them from the clutches of money lenders and loans on the other.

It continued:

This book on Sahara does not explain the fact of how Sahara in its journey of 37 years has become one of the biggest conglomerates of the country just because of the stout business ethics, quality business practices and years of relentless services to its customers and depositors, which has generated faith among crores of our depositors, investors and customers across the country.

The book also forgets to address this core constituent of the story of Sahara India Pariwar, about whom everyone talks but does not venture to know—the very poor depositors who have faith in us and whose hard-earned earnings Sahara is a faithful custodian of, for so many years.

The book at best can be treated as a perspective of the author with all its defamatory content, insinuation and other objections, which prompted us to exercise our right to approach the court of law in order to save the interest of the organization and its crores of depositors and 12 lakh workers.

And ended, ironically, wishing Bandopadhyay the very best:

We are sure that the readers are intelligent enough to see through the maze of plots and appreciate the values that we stand for and the activities we undertake for nation building.

We also wish the author success, though we don't agree with many of the things and the way they were presented in the book.

This was possibly the first time that a book had been published that included such a disavowing disclaimer from the subject at hand. So, did it harm the credibility of the writer? Did the 'compromise' work out better for the Sahara India Pariwar than it had for the journalist who had undertaken such painstaking research?

A statement issued by the group asserted, 'In line with the best traditions of Sahara and as a gesture of our respect for a journalist's freedom, we had withdrawn our case against the publication of the book. But we have put forward our objections and reservations in the form of a disclaimer in the book and we are sure that the readers are intelligent enough to see through the maze of plots and appreciate the values that we stand for and the activities we undertake for the sake of nation building.'

Bandopadhyay was more forthright: 'I think this is probably the first instance in Indian publishing history of using such a disclaimer. The decision to display it prominently was my publisher's to get publicity for the book. I guess this generates interest, curiosity among readers. To that extent, it has helped the book sell more. I have seen at airport bookstalls people buying the book after reading the disclaimer. Has it helped the group to explain its point of view? I don't know the answer.'

A lot of information about both Roy and Sahara were already in the public domain when *Sahara: The Untold Story* was published. What Bandopadhyay had added were behind-the-scenes details, and a contextualisation of the complicated issue of RNBCs. 'With honesty and sincerity, I tried to reveal the mystery that shrouded the group through painstaking research. Has any newspaper or magazine ever reported what transpired at the meetings that the RBI held at its headquarters with Roy in the run-up to the clamp down on his RNBC? The book says all that, with graphic details, as if I were present at those meetings. It also gives an insider perspective of Sahara's fight with market regulator SEBI. These are only two examples. The book is filled with many incidents and anecdotes that were not there in the public domain. Have I been able to accomplish what I aspired for? Probably not. But the book has raised many pertinent questions and created a context for future research on the Sahara group.'

Bandopadhyay had also gone beyond Sahara and dealt with the murky subject of shadow banking. There was one entire chapter on the Kolkata-based Peerless group, another large RNBC—its rise and fall and revival. "Unlike Sahara, which I had been following for years as a journalist, Peerless was not on my radar till the time I started researching for the Sahara book. Since Peerless too, like Sahara, was a RNBC, and probably as big as Sahara at some point of time, I thought I must include Peerless too in the book even though it was a very different kind of organisation in terms of business philosophy. I met the Peerless boss SK Roy, former chairman DN Ghosh[13] and Dipankar Basu who replaced Ghosh as chairman, and board director SM Datta and many others to understand Peerless.'

---

13 For reference to DN Ghosh, also see chapter: *The Unhappy Prince.*

Still, the most captivating reconstruction in Bandopadhyay's work arguably was that of the RBI team's meetings with Sahara officials on 12 and 16 June 2008. And it was almost as if the writer, as he said, was present at those meetings. Among information not in the public domain was this:

> Like the Sahara team, the RBI team was also taking breaks to discuss the developments and strategies. [P] Krishnamurthy [chief general manager] left the meeting for a few minutes, took the lift and went to the 18th floor where [V] Leeladhar [RBI deputy governor] was waiting patiently.

> When Krishnamurthy returned, the final outlines were discussed and both teams drafted a note on plain paper on the changes to be made in the Sahara board and its auditors. Roy was requested to write down everything on a Sahara letterhead and bring it back the next day. Only after that would the RBI issue a press release. Roy agreed to send the note, but bargained hard to extract a promise from the RBI team that the statement would say that Sahara had volunteered the changes.

> In retrospect, it was a model discussion for both the RBI and Sahara—their teams fought hard on virtually every point but in the end settled it amicably. The RBI established the regulator's supremacy with dignity and Roy gave up his empire with a smile.

> At well past midnight, Leeladhar sent a text message to [YV] Reddy, who had not yet gone to bed, 'Sir, mission completed. Strictly as you wanted.' He dictated the message to Krishnamurthy, who typed it on Leeladhar's mobile while taking the lift down from the 18th floor. 'Great job. God bless you,' Leeladhar's mobile phone flashed back as the deputy governor left the RBI headquarters at 12.30am.

So, if the book had been written after such meticulous research, what prompted Roy to harass Bandopadhyay? 'I did not expect the ₹200 crore defamation suit simply because I had taken Roy into confidence while writing the book. He was in the know that I was writing a book on him, but probably he did not expect me to delve deep and write certain things which possibly don't show the group in a very positive manner. There is a book on Roy in Bengali, published more than a decade ago. Popular Bengali novelist Mani Shankar Mukherjee better known as Shankar wrote it after meeting Roy several times at Aamby Valley. It treated the subject very differently; Roy has been depicted there as the best Bengali entrepreneur ever. Maybe my treatment of the subject (in comparison to Shankar's) had upset Roy and he therefore wanted to block its publication.' Shankar's 2003 biography of Roy was titled *Bangalir Vitta Sadhana: Saharar Itikatha* (A Bengali's Practice of Finance: The Sahara Story).

Most would doubt if Bandopadhyay's 'treatment' had at all been harsh or one-sided, by any measure. In fact, the last chapter of the book started off acknowledging Roy's many positive qualities:

> Had the regulators not been after him, Roy would have done wonders in India. First, the RBI forced him to shut down his residuary non-banking company (RNBC) and then SEBI began breathing down his neck about the optionally fully convertible debentures (OFCDs). Each time, Roy tweaked his business, finding new ways to source money. He isn't one to down the shutters or retire to bask in the glory of his accumulated wealth and friendship among the high and mighty.

But, it was not gratifying either. The chapter that carried excerpts of the interview with the businessman was titled 'The Subrata Roy Myth', and also mentioned how Roy reveled in pomp, splendour and loyalty—which happened to be ingredients in his financial success. 'The glitz and glamour attract the poor; they remain glued to Roy, who straddles the world of glamour and the other India that lives in Gorakhpur, Varanasi and Lucknow with consummate ease.' The book did not try to bolster the cult image that had grown around the man; it attempted to make Roy appear more human:

> Roy clearly knows how to build trust and credibility among the poor, not so much among the regulators. That's probably because he doesn't seem to have faith in regulators—he always shifts from one regulatory regime to another and when one door closes, he finds and opens another in no time.
>
> ...
>
> The group runs some 4,799 establishments—many are being continuously set up for regulatory arbitraging. While the main source of money for the group remains a mystery, this is an established fact. The entrepreneur in him feels claustrophobic in regulations and continuously looks for ways to get on top of things. For some time he succeeds, but ultimately he gets trapped. He is smart enough to open another front by that time.

That chapter was in a way open-ended—for both Roy and Sahara:

> Roy can create mass hysteria. For an outsider, it can look like a theatre of the absurd, but Roy is a master of public theatre—he knows how to reach out to people, excite them and entice them. Even when the SEBI chapter comes to a close, the Sahara show will probably go on.

The show certainly went on, but in the drama that unfolded at a lethargic pace, Roy and his Sahara family members came across as abject caricatures of their former selves—more than two years since he was arrested, Roy still remained behind bars, and the group had not been able to wriggle out of its financial mess. First, Sahara was unable to raise ₹10,000 crore (half in cash, and remaining in bank guarantees) that the Supreme Court asked the group to deposit for bail. Sahara's accounts, blocked a year earlier, were unfrozen and the group was even allowed to sell its properties. Roy was even allowed to use Tihar Jail's guesthouse for 25 days so that he could personally negotiate the sales of his properties abroad, including hotels like the Plaza Hotel in New York and Grosvenor House in London. In January 2015, the court permitted Sahara to seek a loan from abroad to pay Roy's bail money and approved a deal with US-based Mirach Capital. Everything either remained on paper or came across as vacuous rhetoric; nothing worked.

In many ways, there were uncanny similarities between *Sahara: The Untold Story* and the Hamish McDonald book on Dhirubhai Ambani and Reliance Industries Limited (RIL). In both cases, the legal threats to the writers came even before the book had been published. Both were works of narrative non-fiction about men who had built huge empires, and both books were about group companies wherein the fates of millions of investors/depositors depended. Roy's rise in fortunes had been as spectacular as that of Ambani, but where he goofed up was in the display of his sheer arrogance at not giving in even when put on the block by the Supreme Court.

Then there were logistical factors, possibly wicked in intent too. One of the reasons why only rich individuals and corporate entities seek huge amounts as damages when they file defamation suits is because only such individuals and companies can afford to pay ten per cent of the damages sought as court fees. Couple this with the fact that defamation suits can be filed anywhere. The pretext can be that anyone can take umbrage anywhere, and therefore take recourse to the law in any place. Many believe that the main reason why Subrata Roy decided to move the Calcutta High Court against Bandopadhyay is that the Calcutta High Court asks for only

₹10,000 as court fees in defamation cases and not ten per cent which others ask for. Plus, Bandopadhyay would have to shuttle between Kolkata and Mumbai.

All said and done, the book saw the light of day, but its writer was made to go through substantial duress. 'It's not easy for an individual to fight an establishment like Sahara, that too in a city where I don't live. The case was filed in Kolkata where I held the so-called office for profit in the form of HT Media Ltd that owns *Mint*. I didn't have to spend much as my legal firm did not charge me anything; the advance that I got from the publisher took care of the cost of frequent flights to Kolkata and Delhi, local transport and stay. However, it was a tough battle and many advised me to give up the book. I lost weight, got more grey hair. At some point my wife thought I was crazy as no sane person can take up such a fight.'

So, did the legal wrangling affect his work? Did he have second thoughts about the book? And yes, would he do something of that sort again? Bandopadhyay was clear: 'My office was extremely supportive. I was excused from my daily chores, but I never missed the deadline for my Monday column *Banker's Trust*. Yes, it was a tough time, but I never thought of giving up. I reconciled to the fact that one needs to go through such an ordeal when one is writing on a group like Sahara. I approached it as a total package—starting from research to investigation, interviews, accessing documents, writing the book and fighting the court case. Frankly, my spirit was never dented. I will do it again if I get the right subject.'

Bandopadhyay is right. For journalists with a story at hand, the work must go on.

3

Don't Ruia That Decision

In early 2015, a whistleblower went public with internal communications of the Essar group, claiming that those showed undue favours to ministers, bureaucrats and journalists in order to push business interests. On 27 February, the correspondence became the subject matter of a public interest litigation (PIL) filed in the Supreme Court by the Centre for Public Interest Litigation (CPIL). The incident, which came to be popularly referred to as the Essar Leaks case, threw the national capital into a tizzy for a while.

The politicians named in the emails cut across party lines, but the ones who faced the most flak, especially on an uncharitable and truculent social media, were a bunch of journalists. Essar executives had been arranging cabs for some Delhi-based journalists, in one case for 10 days; the company kept a record of all such requests made and granted. There were also references to stories being 'planted' in newspapers as well as questions being 'planted' among 'friendly' journalists at press conferences of ministries such as the steel ministry. Journalists were pampered and indulged across the board.

The emails were a veritable catalogue of allegations. A sampler, this. An Essar group executive from Delhi sent an email to their

Mumbai office on 10 July 2012 with the subject: 'Worth finding out who will carry what tomorrow if possible?' The email read: 'As you are aware we had issued a press release regarding Gujarat government action today... suggest if you can catch hold of desk guys across publications to ensure that headlines for tomorrow's news on this issue is in our favour or at least neutral.' The mail referred to a particular financial daily which was carrying a 'negative' headline and the advice was to 'try to get it mild.'

The politicians nonchalantly carried on as if nothing had happened, but three senior journalists resigned from their jobs after being indicted in the emails, having come across as people who had asked for (out-of-turn) favours from the Essar group. The three were Sandeep Bamzai, editor of *Mail Today*; Anupama Airy, energy editor with *Hindustan Times*; and, Meetu Jain, deputy news editor with the Times Now television channel. Mayur Shekhar Jha, formerly with the Headlines Today channel, was also named for booking a guest house in 2012 when he had asked for arrangements of lunch for 15 guests. He was not employed with any organisation at the time.

Most news items that appeared in the media over that frenzied week were more about people like Nitin Gadkari, Union minister and former president of the Bharatiya Janata Party (BJP), and still more about the journalists mentioned earlier. There was precious little, relatively speaking, that appeared about the Essar group itself. The villains were politicians and journalists, the corporates got away light—well, almost.

Scroll journalist Supriya Sharma, who had earlier been a state correspondent with the *Times of India* newspaper in Chhattisgarh, was among the few who dug out a lot of muck on the group. There were, after all, innumerable references to Chhattisgarh in the mails released into the public domain. And these pertained to Essar Steel, part of the Essar group, which had signed a memorandum of understanding in 2005 with the state government to set up a steel plant in Bastar; in return, Chhattisgarh allowed it access to iron ore through a mining lease. Though neither materialised, Essar Steel kept buying discarded iron ore at discounted rates from the public sector National Mineral Development Corporation (NMDC). These were mixed with water, and the slurry was sent down a 267km-long pipeline to Vishakapatnam in Andhra Pradesh. By doing so, the costs came down to ₹80 per tonne instead of having to transport by rail or road at a more expensive ₹550 per tonne.

But, there was one stumbling block—the pipeline passed through the Maoist-dominated Bastar area. The dots were joined in 2011, when it came to light that the Essar group was paying protection money to Maoists to safeguard its operations in the state. A cable dated 11 January 2010, originating from the US consulate in Mumbai and released by WikiLeaks revealed:

> A senior representative from Essar, a major industrial company with large mining and steel-related facilities in Chhattisgarh, told Congenoff (Consul General Office) that the company pays the Maoists 'a significant amount' not to harm or interfere with their operations. When the Maoists occasionally break this agreement and damage Essar property or threaten personnel, Essar sets different Maoist groups against each other to suppress the situation.

> All the key ingredients are there: the state police are preventing any oversight from civil society groups; the central government has surged large numbers of paramilitary forces unfamiliar with the language, communities, and terrain of the region; state authorities have given a free hand to security forces, who are suspicious that politically-organised tribals may be Maoist sympathisers.

The Maoists and tribals are virtually indistinguishable to outsiders, making it extremely difficult to separate friend from foe; state efforts to recruit tribals as special police officers have stoked intra-tribal conflict, raising civilian casualties; and the Maoists for their part, have proven willing to use opportunistic brutality on civilians and security forces alike, provoking even more cycles of violence.

The company denied the allegations, but only a few days later DVCS Varma, general manager of Essar Steel, was arrested from Kirandul in Dantewada district where the company operated an iron ore beneficiation plant. Varma was arrested under Sections 121 and 124(A) of the Indian Penal Code (IPC) that amounted to waging war against the state and sedition. This followed the arrest of BK Lala, a building contractor with Essar, from a weekly village bazaar on 9 September. The police claimed he was carrying ₹15 lakh, which he confessed he was to deliver to Maoists through one Lingaram Kodopi on behalf of Essar.[14]

An Essar spokesperson denied the charges, stating, 'Such baseless allegations are being made to hurt the image and reputation of the group, which is a law abiding corporate.' But, Lala turned approver in the case in July 2012. It had been Lala who was appointed contractor for repairing the pipeline that was blown up by Maoists in 2009. Lala had it repaired, amid allegations that the company paid off the Maoists. While the company denied the charges, a case was filed against Essar for supporting the Maoists.

But, managing the Maoist ecosystem in Chhattisgarh meant working closely with the local media too. Also mentioned in the

---

14 Activist Soni Sori and her journalist nephew Lingaram Kodopi were arrested on charges of acting as Maoist conduits who had allegedly received protection money for the left-wing rebels from the Essar group in Chhattisgarh.

Essar Leaks mails was one Dev Sharan Tiwari, the bureau chief of the Hindi newspaper *Deshbandhu* in Jagdalpur, the largest town of Bastar.

Essar's senior vice-president Rajamani Krishnamurti wrote in an email on 7 June 2012: 'Mr Tiwari had certain issues about he being discriminated and bypassed in contracts for last two years. He is an influential journalist and can be a big help to us in terms of information and opinion building, if we can encash him to our advantage and at the same time will be great nuisance value if we ignore him.'

Deshbandhu was not too big, but the journalist's brother was: Vidya Sharan Tiwari, the district president of the Bharatiya Janata Party (BJP). The reporter became Essar's 'eyes and ears' in the region, and for his cooperation, Tiwari was rewarded with a transportation contract, a subsequent email in November said.

Supriya Sharma wrote:

> Speaking with *Scroll*, Tiwari denied taking contracts from Essar. 'I used to meet the PR officials when they would visit,' he said. 'But I did not take any business from them.' When asked if he had a transport business, he said he used to have one, but it folded up many years ago.

> The editor-in-chief of *Deshbandhu*, Lalit Surjan, expressed shock at the allegations. 'This is news to me. I'm hearing about this from you,' he said. 'Dev Sharan Tiwari has been a very good correspondent. At the time of the Essar case [over alleged payments to Maoists], he did objective reporting. Since our newspaper has limited resources, and we cannot afford to recruit full-time high-salaried journalists at all places, we do not see anything wrong if our journalists solicit advertisements for the paper, for which they earn commissions above their salaries. But we do not allow them to accept contracts for their businesses.'

Given the backdrop to the Essar Leaks incident, it was rather unbecoming of most media establishments not to probe deep, and quarry out the bigger story. After all, the Essar group had been named both in the 2G Spectrum Scam[15] relating to misallocation and mis-pricing of second-generation electromagnetic spectrum used for telecommunication as well as the Coal Scam on irregular allotment of coal-bearing blocks to private companies. There was a story somewhere, buried under the overflowing scams.

Even while sparks were flying over the Essar Leaks episode, the Essar group was making rounds of the courts. In December 2011, the country's top investigating agency—the Central Bureau of Investigation (CBI)—charged five officials of the Essar group and Loop Telecom with fraud and conspiracy as part of the wide-ranging court-monitored investigation into the ₹1,76,000 crore 2G Spectrum Scam. The charges were against industrialists Ravi Ruia and Anshuman Ruia, promoters of the Essar group, its director for strategy and planning, Vikas Saraf, and Loop promoters IP Khaitan and Kiran Khaitan. The accused also included three companies—Loop Telecom Pvt Ltd, Loop Mobile India Ltd and Essar Tele Holding. The charges were filed under Section 120 B, which defines criminal conspiracy, and Section 420, cheating, of the Indian Penal Code (IPC).

The moot point of the CBI was that Loop was part of the Essar group and had, therefore, obtained telecom licences it was not entitled to, as the Ruia-controlled group simultaneously owned

---

15 **Disclosure:** Paranjoy Guha Thakurta was one of many concerned citizens who joined a public interest litigation in the 2G Spectrum Scam, originally filed by the Centre for Public Interest Litigation (CPIL) led by lawyer Prashant Bhushan. Guha Thakurta has written extensively on the scam, with the first article on the subject appearing in the *Economic Times* in November 2007. Soon after its publication, a legal notice was served on him by Reliance Communications.

33 per cent of Vodafone-Essar. The argument was that the Essar group had violated telecom licence conditions that prohibited mobile companies from holding more than 10 per cent stake in two service providers. The rule was known as 'Clause 8', after the relevant section in mobile licence rules. What had landed the Essar group in a spot was a family connection—Kiran Khaitan was the sister of Essar group founders and promoters Shashi and Ravi Ruia, and was based in Dubai along with her husband IP Khaitan.

The CBI did not press for bribery charges; it merely said the telecom firm bagged licences for 21 circles for nearly ₹1,450 crore but didn't bribe any public servant for the purpose. Loop was an ineligible company which got licences; it was alleged to have manipulated the policy. The chargesheet, running into 105 pages and over 22,000 annexures, alleged that the Essar group used Loop as a front company to acquire telecom licences in 2008. The licences were given during the tenure of sacked telecom minister Andimuthu Raja, the prime accused in the 2G Spectrum Scam.

The Essar group issued denials, and even unsuccessfully appealed to the Supreme Court to grant a stay on the summonses issued against group officials. It remained at the receiving end in the courts. In June 2015, Special CBI Judge OP Saini dismissed Anshuman Ruia's plea in which he sought permission to travel abroad for business purposes and certain family commitments. Saini said names of the countries, to be visited by the accused, were not mentioned in his application and 'the court is left to grapple with the itinerary to find out the countries which would be visited by the accused.' That was not all—the judge even said, 'I also find that documents attached with the application are also abstruse and obscure and it is very difficult to make any sense out of them,' the judge said, adding, 'It is thus clear that the application has been filed just to waste the time of the court and not so much for seeking permission to travel abroad.'

In December 2015, the Supreme Court held that the company and its promoters Ravi and Anshuman Ruia would have to be tried by the special 2G trial court, while it dismissed their petitions challenging the jurisdiction of the 2G court to try them in a case arising out of the probe in the 2G Spectrum Scam.

One magazine saw the bigger picture. Vinod K Jose, editor of the *Caravan* magazine that specialises in long-form narrative journalism, decided to take on the story. In fact, as Jose was to later tell the writers of this book, the magazine was already working on the story at the time; Krishn Kaushik was assigned to the job. For months, from digging out facts and sifting through allegations, and of course putting in a lot of legwork, Kaushik came up with a 10,000-plus-word story. That's when the sh*t hit the proverbial fan.

The *Caravan* started rolling out its series of stories from 2 June 2015 through Vantage, its web-exclusive section. The initial stories took off from the Essar Leaks mails. The first was about how the *Sunday Guardian* newspaper, whose editor MJ Akbar was to later join the BJP. The weekly newspaper had approached the company for advertisements in its Gujarat supplement that was published on 8 January 2012. It bandied a letter of endorsement from the state information department, and the newspaper's chief operating officer Kamal Shah had written: 'We will also be highlighting that chief minister Mr Narendra Modi will one day transform India into an economic superpower.' Akbar too wrote a letter to Shashi Ruia asking for the group to advertise in the supplement. Initially Essar was hesitant, but gave in on seeing the Modi card.

The company responded to Kaushik's query about the incident with an officialese response: 'As regards Essar's participation in the supplement published by *Sunday Guardian*, we wish to clarify that the same was done to promote Essar's infrastructure business in the ordinary course of business and not at the behest of any person whomsoever.' After this episode, Modi distanced himself from the Essar group.

The monthly was piecing things together that no other journalistic establishment had done, especially given that the Essar group had remained in the news for one reason or another. The Essar Leaks incident, in fact, had followed close on the heels of a sensational series of arrests related to suspected corporate espionage that were made in New Delhi only a week or so earlier. A number of people were arrested, including Essar deputy general manager Vinay Kumar, for buying confidential documents from two former staffers of the ministry of petroleum and natural gas. Police sources were quoted saying that every presentation made by foreign firms to the petroleum ministry was leaked out to Indian corporate houses for a hefty price. 'The ministry got alarmed about such operations after a foreign company complained that it would not make any more presentations owing to the fears of information leak. Several firms from abroad also realised that their presentations were being re-presented by some Indian corporates.'

The magazine went on to connect the dots in pointing out how Essar was accessing government documents that impacted its businesses. A 4 June 2015 story linked Essar Leaks with the corporate espionage case. All this while, Essar had been putting up a brave face and insisting that it abided by the laws of the land.

But Kaushik reported:

However, it appears now that Essar's concern about the privacy of its internal documents does not extend to sensitive documents—that could directly or indirectly affect the company's various businesses—belonging to the government. Although the petroleum leaks in February 2015 resulted in the arrest of only one mid-level executive from Essar, a new set of emails that have been released by the whistleblower reveal that no matter who gained access to those documents, they were exchanged among the top officers of the company. In fact, the process that was set in place by the company to access government documents appears to be so sophisticated that Essar seemed to be able to get specific documents pertaining to matters that could affect or benefit its business decisions at will.

The report said that the influence of the executives of this group did not seem to be restricted to just the petroleum and finance ministries—it extended to the crucial coal ministry as well.

It appears from these and previously released emails, most of which are from 2012 and 2013, that the group's executives appeared to enjoy uninhibited access in the ministries including, but probably not restricted to, finance, coal, petroleum, environment, steel, railways and shipping, all of which have direct impact on the multiple industries that Essar has a prominent presence in. The audacity of some of these emails, wherein senior executives from the company demand that its officers acquire copies of sensitive government documents, betrays a sense of entitlement. Requests for documents, drafts and copies either flowed from the top or were pre-empted, as mid-level executives appeared to send whatever documents they were able to access and could potentially be relevant, to their bosses. A former petroleum secretary told me that any leak is 'undesirable' for any government, irrespective of its contents.

The next was a straight-jacket, innocuous report on email exchanges among Pradeep Gupta, private secretary to President Pranab Mukherjee; Adil Malia, group president for human resources (HR); Sunil Bajaj, director of corporate relations at Essar Services India Limited (ESIL); Rahul Taneja, senior vice-president and head of corporate human resources with the group; Lynne Sampson, an HR manager with Essar Oil in London; and Alok Chauhan, a corporate affairs executive at ESIL. The emails from September 2013 onwards indicated that the President's granddaughter Suchismita Mukherjee could be hired at Essar's London office, and a trail mail wondered whether they should employ her as an intern or as a full-timer.

And then *Caravan*, on 20 and 21 July put out lists of bureaucrats, journalists and politicians who had been handed out iPads as Diwali gifts in 2010. The *Caravan* reporters contacted the nine journalists who figured in the list. Some of them confirmed that iPads had indeed been delivered but that they had returned them, others denied that any such delivery had been made. The magazine's second list named politicians. The entire list was uploaded on to the website; the names of those still being or not been contacted were blurred out.

Reporters Kaushik, Atul Dev and Ishan Marvel wrote:

> The names in this list, as well as the procedure used to contact and deliver a Diwali gift to these individuals, reveals the thought and effort that Essar had invested in cultivating influence amongst those in positions of power. The politicians on the list range across the political spectrum, from Ahmed Patel in the Congress to Arun Jaitley in the Bharatiya Janata Party (BJP). Most important political formations in the country are represented by the names on the list—Praful Patel of the Nationalist Congress Party (NCP), SC Mishra of the Bahujan Samaj Party (BSP), Akhilesh Yadav of the Samajwadi Party, Sitaram Yechury of the Communist Party of India—Marxist [CPI(M)] and Mukul Roy of the All India Trinamool Congress (TMC).

Of the twenty-two politicians who were contacted, only one politician—former minister of state for defence MM Pallam Raju of the Congress—admitted that he had received the gift.

The iPad story was incidental—it was something the magazine came across while working on the main story. But as Jose said, 'It had a novelty and curiosity factor—about how a company works with influential people.' The work—that of contacting all the 195 people mentioned in the lists—was distributed between two reporters for about a week. It was not humanly possible to elicit responses from one and all. They gave up after a point, but did incorporate the denials/confirmations from those who could be contacted.

The publication of the lists finally got Essar reacting. In a legal notice dated 21 July, an advocate representing Essar Services India Pvt Ltd, wrote that the contents of the article were defamatory, vicious and written recklessly. The advocate wrote, among other things:

> That you the noticees are spreading false rumours about the conduct and reputation of my client and are indulging in fuelling a controversy with the intention not only to malign the reputation of my client but also to gain publicity of your magazine.

> The acts committed by you noticees are reflective of the unethical practices perpetuated by you by furthering sensational and frivolous/baseless journalism for furthering your commercial interests in gaining publicity and higher ratings for your online magazine, and the same are in violation of the code of conduct and journalistic ethics for which my client will be forced to initiate against you in terms of the Press Council Act, 1978.

The response from the *Caravan* went four days later, and noted that Essar had not denied the existence of the list of people or the emails themselves. Among what the magazine's lawyer said in response was a paragraph that is crucial to the argument that this book seeks to underline:

> That by publishing an independent monthly magazine, my clients are playing a critical role in our democracy through exercising and upholding the fundamental right to freedom of speech and expression guaranteed under Article 19(1)(a) of the Indian Constitution. The article published by my clients is an exercise of freedom of speech and expression on their part. As the article deals with a subject that is of public importance, by publishing the truth and their honest opinion and reasonably verified facts my clients have advanced the fundamental right of all citizens to know and be informed. On all such matters of public interest and public importance, the media has a right and duty to report and the public has a right to know, and the same cannot constitute defamation or any other crime in law.

The response also emphasised on the public's right to know:

> My clients have published the article in exercise of their fundamental rights guaranteed under the Constitution of India. It is also worth noting that courts have held that freedom of expression which includes freedom of the press has a capacious content and is not restricted to expression of thoughts and ideas which are accepted and acceptable but also those which offend or shock any section of the population. It also includes the right to receive information and ideas of all kinds from different sources. In essence, the freedom of expression embodies the right to know.

Incidentally, a copy of Essar's notice was also sent to one Delhi Press Club. As the *Caravan* noted in its response: 'That the outset, there is no such entity as 'Delhi Press Club' mentioned as noticee no. 4 in the legal notice in existence at the address mentioned against noticee no. 4. My clients are neither aware nor associated with Delhi Press Club which has been stated to be present at the registered address of Delhi Press Patra Prakashan Pvt Ltd. You are therefore, requested to ask your clients to verify their facts.'

The magazine did not get bogged down. Three days after its response, the *Caravan* published an elaborate article by independent journalist Pranati Mehra that went on to assert that allegations being made against Essar were not confined to granting of favours and gifts; the rot was deeper:

> A showcause notice issued by the directorate of revenue intelligence (DRI), Mumbai, against the company in March this year indicates that Essar may have been siphoning off money from India through its network of companies abroad. The group has allegedly creamed off foreign exchange of over ₹2,600 crore. It has done this through imports of equipment for its power companies. A copy of the 247-page notice is in the *Caravan's* possession.

> The notice—signed by PK Dash, the additional director-general of the DRI—contains diagrams that illustrate the maze of companies that the group invested in, formed, or bought in Dubai, Mauritius, Cyprus, the United Kingdom and [the] Cayman Islands. It also includes tabulated information on the import consignments that were used to siphon the money, their values and the invoices.

It was, of course, as even Essar officials themselves said, only a notice: 'We strongly refute the allegations in the showcause notice. We state that the project cost compares favourably with similar projects built in India... This is only a showcause notice and the company's confident that during the proceedings, the explanations provided will be considered satisfactory by the adjudicating authorities.'

It was not a conviction, but was damning enough. Mehra concluded: 'The DRI's showcause notice indicates deliberate malpractice by the Essar group. The agency's findings deserve an extended investigation by the enforcement directorate and tax authorities of India.'

All this while, the fact that the *Caravan* was working on a story about Essar was already doing the rounds in Delhi. The magazine was known for its irreverent long-form cover stories, and if it was about Essar, it would certainly be big. At least, that's what the grapevine of the national capital believed. Jose and others at the *Caravan* would get friendly phone calls from journalists enquiring about the work in progress. There was also a buzz about how the company was trying to get appointments with Jose and other staff members at the *Caravan*. This happened at a time that the eventual cover story was still months away from being written. The interest in the yet-to-be-written story was so much that a gossip column in the *Mumbai Mirror* even wrote about how a magazine that specialised in long-form journalism was feverishly working on a story about the Essar group. The column also spoke of how the company was reportedly trying to influence the story. The story was news already.

The reporter concerned had not yet got in touch with senior officials of the group. This was standard practice. For these kind of stories, a journalist does not go straight up to the company— unless and till the reporter has a fair hold on the material. That crucial contact with the main protagonist of a story is usually staved off till the last month of reporting, so that other ground is covered over the first 3–4 months.

There was a pressing reason why the *Caravan* decided to do the Essar story. As Jose explained, 'There was in a sense, a kind of business practices that the company was involved in which needed scrutiny. Moreover, here was a company whose name was dragged into all the major scams (from 2G Spectrum Scam to Coal Scam). This was a company which had pulled through political changes too. There were operations of the company outside of Delhi which needed to be looked at as well. It was an ambitious story.' Running parallelly with the name-cropping in the scams, one also saw that the Essar group was partnering with media companies in supporting their festivals or events. 'There was naturally some curiosity from our end to look at the company in an in-depth way.' The motive was only to put the spotlight on a company that had hitherto escaped public scrutiny.

The blockbuster—a riveting and in-depth 14,300-word article— conclusively came in the form of the August 2015 cover story 'Purchasing Power: How Essar Wields Influence Over Indian Government and Finance'. The same story was titled 'Doing the Needful: Essar's Industry of Influence' in the online version (which was released on the website after the usual print-online time-lag of about 15 days).

As the writer Kaushik began penning the Essar saga, he wrote of the company's debts:

> Chronic indebtedness, accompanied by a lack of transparency, is by no means new to the world of Indian enterprise. Many firms comparable to Essar in size are deep in the red, and Essar is not the first company to cause alarm among its observers. Yet, in spite of its successes in the last decade, the company has never wholly regained its reputation. In my attempts to investigate the group this summer, which covered Mumbai and Delhi as well as rural Madhya Pradesh and Chhattisgarh, I found persistent support for the charge that the Ruia family was, above all, out to protect its own interests over those of its lenders and shareholders, or of those whose lives stand to be permanently affected by the

group's pursuit of land and resources. That accusation is further substantiated by the emails now called the Essar Leaks.

If the company was so much in the red, what was it doing about the same? Kaushik pointed out:

Everyone I spoke to who has researched or tracked Essar's actions, both in India and abroad, told me that none of Essar's problems are unique. Companies such as the Adani Group and Reliance Anil Dhirubhai Ambani Group, a breakaway corporation led by Mukesh's younger brother, have acquired loans worth ₹80,000 crore to over a lakh crore each. The story of how the Ruias manage their behemoth of a company today has parallels in most of the country's large corporate groups. Still, several of my interviewees in Mumbai unconsciously echoed each other when they said, 'These guys'—Essar—'have taken it to another level.'

And that's what the cover story was about: the way Essar held sway over politicians and other influencers. The story prompted another legal notice, one that was dated 8 August.

The magazine replied ten days later, pointing out that the story was 'based on the facts provided by the whistleblower' who was an employee of Essar and whose leaked documents were used by eminent lawyer Prashant Bhushan in a public interest litigation in the Supreme Court in addition to 'extensive research, investigation and interviews' by staff reporter Kaushik. The response also said that 'several crucial facts' in the story were never rebutted by Essar: from the exact debts accumulated by various entities of the Essar group and their promoters to the allegations from villagers in the state of Chhattisgarh accusing Essar of illegally acquiring land for its projects; and from various people having been given jobs within the Essar group on the recommendation of politicians, bureaucrats and journalists, to Essar producing a monthly information system report wherein action plans included recommendations such as suppressing an issue or arranging favourable reports from various government departments. The lawyer representing *Caravan* wrote: 'In view of the admitted position, the allegations and contentions made in your legal notice are an afterthought, baseless, false, wrong and frivolous.'

Essar responded the following day, 19 August, filing a civil defamation suit of ₹250 crore on the *Caravan*: 'a genuine pre-estimate of the damages suffered... considering 'Essar' has investments in various sectors...across five continents and the worldwide goodwill and reputation that it holds.'

Essar sought a temporary injunction and *ex parte* order to restrain the defendants from 'in any manner publishing, issuing, circulating, distributing or advertising in any manner whatsoever either in print or electronic or any other form of media any defamatory story or article concerning the plaintiff,' claiming that there is a 'clear cut and strong *prima facie* case' against *Caravan*. 'If the reliefs as prayed for herein are granted, no harm, loss, injury or prejudice will be caused to the defendants. However, if the same are not granted, the plaintiff will suffer irreparable harm, loss and injury, which cannot be compensated in terms of money,' it said, listing 12 statements and/or comments that the company alleged were '*per se* defamatory... without the least justification.'

The defamation case had its Streisand Effect too. According to the *Newslaundry* website, the cover story on Essar generated, on an average, twice the amount of traffic it got on the day the article was released online. If the intention had been to minimise critical reportage, it had clearly not worked to Essar's favour. So, was there more to the defamation suit than met the eye?

After all, the case was filed, of all places, in faraway Ahmedabad. The *Caravan's* publisher—Delhi Press Patra Prakashan Ltd—

moved the Supreme Court seeking to transfer the case out of the Ahmedabad city court to one in Delhi. Prashant Bhushan, who represented the magazine, argued that none of the actions leading to the alleged defamation had occurred in Ahmedabad, and the appropriate and convenient forum was Delhi. He described the petition as a strategic litigation against public participation (SLAPP) suit aimed at harassing the magazine. Bhushan contended that it was in the interest of justice to transfer the case to Delhi, so that *Caravan* could produce its witnesses and defend its case.

A two-member bench of the court, however, on 8 September 2015 declined to transfer the case. The court instead directed the *Caravan* to file its response in the Ahmedabad court. There was a saving grace, though—the bench granted the *Caravan* the liberty to approach the apex court at a later stage, if the situation arose.

Meanwhile, something strange happened in Delhi. Midway through the first week of August, copies of the magazine started disappearing from the market—a tad too fast. On one occasion, a distributor of the magazine in South Delhi asked for an additional supply of 500 copies. This particular tranche was tracked—from the moment it left the magazine's premises in Jhandewalan Estate in central Delhi to the distributor's at Nehru Place in the south. The lot was picked up by two men in an autorickshaw, which first made for Defence Colony, then Khan Market, and trundled around for 2–3 hours before finally stopping in front of the residence of the Ruias on the posh Lodhi Road. This is only hearsay, of course.

As the case ambled on, Essar remained in the news. The *Indian Express* which had carried a series of reports on the Essar Leaks case kept following up the litigation that had been filed by the CPIL. In December 2015, the newspaper reported on a 19-slide presentation titled 'Navigating the corridors of Power: To positively influence the high and mighty', made on 19 February 2010 by its director, corporate relations, Sunil Bajaj. Its opening line was: 'The quality of your life is the quality of your relationships.'

Every time the newspaper carried a story, it included stock responses from the company. In an August 2015 article, the Essar group was reported saying, 'The questions are *sub judice*[16] and we, therefore, refrain from giving our response. Nothing stated by us herein should, however, be construed as an admission of all or any of your allegations made. We reiterate and say that Essar is a responsible corporate and we adhere to the highest standards of governance and ethics.'

The *Indian Express* had already been threatened by Essar for publishing the news stories based on the whistleblower's emails way back in February. The company had then said in a statement:

> Stealing emails constitutes theft and as you would be aware that Delhi Police is taking strong steps against persons stealing information... We have already filed an appropriate complaint with the concerned authorities...

> If you do take to publishing any allegations based on any email stolen from the system, we would take appropriate steps, including by way of a criminal complaint of theft and, it would then be obvious that you would be a receiver of stolen property.

> Arrests have been made by Delhi Police of persons who have allegedly received 'stolen property' by way of purloined documents [in the corporate espionage case]. We would take appropriate legal steps to ensure that the protection of law available against theft in all its forms is extended to our property, i.e. our servers and data on these servers.

---

16 In law, *sub judice*, Latin for 'under judgment', means that a particular case or matter is under trial or being considered by a judge or court. Matters are considered to be *sub judice* once legal proceedings become active.

The question arose whether the *Indian Express* was on the right side of the law. A perspective was provided by the *LegallyIndia* website, which reports on Indian legal matters. It recollected the 2014 debate over the leak of internal emails from Sony Pictures, which had been stolen by hackers, with wide disagreements in the public over whether publishing the stolen emails was wrong or necessary. The website spoke of a 2001 US Supreme Court decision which had ruled in favour of a radio station that broadcast an illegally intercepted cellphone conversation between labour officials over teacher salaries. Meanwhile, the Essar Leaks mails remained central to the litigation that the CPIL was pursuing in the Supreme Court.

Essar's reaction to the coverage of the Essar Leaks mails as well as the *Caravan* article was understandable: the group didn't come across squeaky clean. As it is, the Essar group had a history—not too back in the past—of taking legal action against whoever went against the company's desired image.

The Essar group on 28 January 2014 had filed a ₹500 crore defamation suit against Greenpeace India and others in the Bombay High Court over a giant banner unfurled on the front of the conglomerate's headquarters in Mumbai that read 'We kill forests'. Fourteen Greenpeace activists had scaled the building in central Mumbai six days earlier, and unfurled the banner to protest the company's mining plans in Madhya Pradesh, which the activists contended would damage one of India's oldest forests. Incidentally, Kaushik's cover story had kicked off with the Greenpeace protest that had riled the Ruias no end.

The high court that day asked Greenpeace India to remove from its websites, posters, leaflets and pamphlets the alleged defamatory content saying the environmental group was *prima facie* tarnishing the image of a well-known business house; the organisation complied. But its executive director Samit Aich declared in a statement, 'While we respect the observations of the court, we are confident we will prove all charges pressed by Essar wrong in the court of law. Right to protest is fundamental to democracy. We have protested in the most peaceful way and will defend our rights. It is not Greenpeace that is defaming the company but it is the company, their actions and their ways of doing business that is bringing shame on them.'

Greenpeace was soon to wage its own lonely battle against the might of the Indian government. In early June that year, the Intelligence Bureau (IB) had filed a report—the second in about a month, which described Greenpeace as 'a threat to national economic security.'[17] On 16 June, the Essar group tried to encash this IB report in its defamation case against Greenpeace, even as it took on the NGO parallelly in a Madhya Pradesh sessions court in another case. The IB report had also stated that Greenpeace 'actively aided and led by foreign activists visiting India' was violating provisions of the Foreign Contribution (Regulation) Act of 2010 (FCRA), and financing 'sympathetic studies' at the Tata Institute of Social Sciences (TISS) and at the Indian Institute of Technology (IIT), Delhi.

Greenpeace, in any case, had not let down the tempo of its protests. The legal coordinator for campaigns and actions at Greenpeace International, Karianne Bruning, blogged on 23 May:

---

17 **Disclosure:** One of the author's of this book, Paranjoy Guha Thakurta's name finds place in the Intelligence Bureau (IB) report for receiving financial support from Greenpeace for the making of a film titled *Coal Curse: The political economy of coal-based energy in India*, which is available for public viewing on YouTube (http://bit.ly/1Vp6iGt). Guha Thakurta went on to join the board of Greenpeace India, a post he held at the time of publication of this book.

Essar dragged Greenpeace India into court instead of having an open and public debate about Essar's responsibility for destroying the forest, forging documents and putting pressure on local communities. Essar requested a permanent injunction prohibiting further protests on or within 500m from Essar's premises, a gag order and ₹500 crore—approximately 60 million euros—for an alleged damage to their reputation. Pending a hearing where Greenpeace India will provide evidence to substantiate its statements, a Bombay judge granted a temporary injunction on further protests and a gag order. But this hasn't stopped Greenpeace India from exposing the truth.

It hasn't stopped Essar's scare tactics either; in April the company filed another request for a permanent injunction and gag order, claiming that Greenpeace India interfered with the work on site of the Mahan coal mine project as well as allegedly threatening workers (with use of violence). However, 48 hours after a peaceful protest by the local communities at the Mahan site it was four activists who were arrested in the middle of the night, thrown in prison and charged with serious offences. Three of the four detainees have now been released on bail, but one person is still in detention.

Incidentally, Essar was accusing Greenpeace of defamation, even as it was itself being grilled by the Central Bureau of Investigation (CBI) for its role in the Coal Scam. There was the Mahan angle here too—the Mahan Coal block was allocated to Mahan Coal Ltd (a joint venture of Essar Power and Hindalco) in 2006. In 2012, Mahan received the Stage I clearance (in principle), which meant 36 conditions had to be fulfilled before Stage II clearance could be granted. One of the conditions was implementation of the Scheduled Tribes and Other Traditional Forest Dwellers (Recognition of Forest Rights) Act, 2006, better known as the

Forest Rights Act. On 12 February 2014, the Veerappa Moily-led environment ministry granted the Stage II clearance to the block.

Essar claimed to have fulfilled all the 36 conditions, but Greenpeace alleged that the gram sabha (village council) resolution, which formed the basis of the clearance, had been forged. Some villagers, whose signatures appeared in the document, were said to have been dead for years.

The Singrauli case didn't make any headway for Essar. On 7 August 2015, the Supreme Court stayed the trial court proceedings in the defamation case against Greenpeace activist Priya Pillai and two others. A bench of Justice Jagdish Singh Khehar and Justice Adarsh Kumar Goel also issued notices to the company and the Centre on Pillai's plea in which she also challenged the validity of Section 499 (defamation) of the IPC. Pillai contested the defamation complaint on the ground that Essar had filed it to curb freedom of expression and prevent her from raising a voice against the alleged wrongs of the company.

The *Caravan* story on Essar is arguably the most representative of the cases that have been highlighted in this book. It is as much about crony capitalism as it is about media management. It is as much about circumventing of laws as it is about scavenging around in conflict zones.

4

Grabbing A Headline

The Indian media traditionally held in high esteem businessmen of Indian origin and Indian entrepreneurs who exported or conducted business outside. They were either people who brought good name to the country or much-needed foreign exchange, often both; their feathers were not meant to be ruffled. And once outsourcing boomed in the 1990s, this particular class of businesses became the holy cows of the media who were never meant to be rubbed the wrong way. Many of them were of course clean, some not so. In-depth stories about the conduct and the very operations of such people were hard to come by.

Even as more corporate houses came increasingly under the scanner of journalists who wanted to probe stories that went beyond the dour headlines, many Indian businesses became embroiled in controversies over alleged land-grabbing during the second tenure (2009–2014) of Manmohan Singh as Prime Minister of the Congress-led United Progressive Alliance (UPA) government. As pitched battles were sometimes fought between villagers whose lands were said to have been grabbed and police forces who were deployed to protect the interests of the government and its corporate partners, almost all reports of the trampling of civil rights of farmers emanated from within the country itself. There were far too many reports of this kind, and were either too big-scale or too controversial to be ignored by a rather business-friendly media. But, when the *Guardian* newspaper of the United Kingdom (UK) carried a report on 21 March 2011 by the daily's environment editor, John Vidal about Indian investors being among scores of others warding Ethiopians off their ancestral lands, it made little noise in India, lost as it was in the din of the incensed anti-corruption protests that then had India on the boil.

Vidal's report, not particularly damning, spoke of the sparsely-populated Gambella province along the border with Sudan being at the centre of a global rush for cheap land that had been precipitated by the oil price rise of 2007–2008. Many countries, afflicted by food riots, encouraged entrepreneurs to invest abroad to grow food. The Ethiopian government of Meles Zenawi, an ally in the US 'war against terror', had responded to this need by putting 1.1 million hectares of farmland on offer to investors. The *Guardian* article spoke of forests across hundreds of square kilometres being 'felled and burned to the dismay of locals and environmentalists concerned about the fate of the region's rich wildlife.' Villages were being herded together, and farmers were either not being compensated or were having to wait for eternity to be paid off. The story of the glaring rights violations came with the token official denials.

Only one corporation was quoted in the entire story: Bengaluru-based Karuturi Global which was leased land practically at a pittance—just £150 a week for 2,500 sq km of fertile land. Vidal contextualised the size of the land for his British readers, putting it across as an area the size of Dorset county in south-west England. For Indians, that would have been more than one-and-half times the size of the state of Delhi. Karuturi Global had not even seen the land when it was given on a platter by the Ethiopian government, but lapped it up to grow and export palm oil, sugar, rice and other food items.

'It's very good land. It's quite cheap. In fact it is very cheap. We have no land like this in India,' says Karmjeet Sekhon, project manager for what is expected to be one of Africa's largest farms. 'There you are lucky to get 1% of organic matter in the soil. Here it is more than 5%. We don't need fertilisers or herbicides. There is absolutely nothing that will not grow on it.

'To start with there will be 20,000 hectares of oil palm, 15,000 hectares of sugar cane and 40,000 hectares of rice, edible oils and maize and cotton. We are building reservoirs, dykes, roads, towns of 15,000 people. This is phase one. In three years time we will have 300,000 hectares cultivated and maybe 60,000 workers. We could feed a nation here.'

Four days after Vidal's news-breaker came a more indicting one from IRIN, a humanitarian news agency not at all known for any contentious reportage. The Integrated Regional Information Networks (IRIN), as its mandate, 'focused on humanitarian stories from regions often forgotten, under-reported, misunderstood or ignored,' and was a project of the United Nations Office for the Coordination of Humanitarian Affairs (OCHA). IRIN had been established after the 1994 Rwandan genocide, and was headquartered in the Kenyan capital of Nairobi. The agency, now known just by the acronym IRIN after it became independent of the United Nations, often reported from adjacent Ethiopia in the north.

The IRIN focus was clear about the Ethiopian government's land-leasing policy and its impact on people:

The policy, part of a five-year Growth and Transformation Plan, has led to the cheap leasing of thousands of square kilometres of what the government says is mostly under-used or uncultivated land. Officially, land in Ethiopia is government-owned but occupants have customary rights.

Detractors complain of forcible relocation of local pastoralist populations, poorly paid work on the new farms, environmental degradation and a failure to deliver on promises of better infrastructure.

Supplemented with denials from officialdom, this report too quoted only one corporation that was in the thick and thin of things: Karuturi Global. IRIN went beyond the *Guardian* story and talked of infringement of pastoralists' rights since according to the Ethiopian constitution pastoralists 'have the right to free land for grazing and cultivation as well as the right not to be displaced from their own lands.'

'We are pastoralists. How can we stay here for more than three or four months?' asked one villager.

'Karuturi and the government promised us that we will get better jobs, better living conditions but so far they have done nothing other than taking our land and driving us to severe poverty,' he added.

'My community doesn't hate the foreign companies [Karuturi] here. But we want them to be [responsive] to our problems as they have taken our land and our promises are not fulfilled,' he said.

'They are paying us very little money 12 birr [$0.73] a day. When Karuturi Farms took our land we were promised 25 to 30 birr [$1.50-$1.80] per day. They are not paying what they are supposed to pay. We are deceived either by our government and/or by Karuturi,' he said.

Both the *Guardian* and IRIN stories came in the backdrop of an extensive study that the US-based think-tank Oakland Institute (OI) was working on. The Oakland Institute and the Solidarity Movement for a New Ethiopia (SMNE) released on 8 June their joint report on Ethiopia, as part of the larger study on *Understanding Land Investment Deals in Africa*. They looked at 'government-executed land investment deals with foreign investors that give them the rights to some of the most fertile, water-accessible land in Ethiopia for up to 99 years at prices as low as $1.19 per hectare; all done without consulting the people.' It was immaculate documentation that bolstered the cases built by the IRIN and *Guardian* articles.

The researchers discovered that the Land Rent Contractual Agreements for land leases between the Federal Democratic Republic of Ethiopia (FDRE) and 24 companies or individuals had been carried out behind closed doors by the one-party government (Ethiopian People's Revolutionary Democratic Front—EPRDF) of strongman Meles Zenawi:

> Ethiopian citizens are denied the right of private land ownership, but what is essentially 'lifetime land ownership' through these long-term lease agreements are now being given to foreign investors by this cash-strapped government; now being accused of laundering 8.2 billion dollars. As this land is leased, hundreds of thousands of some of the most vulnerable and marginalized Ethiopians are being forced from their indigenous land and told to build new homes within designated areas provided by the regime; purportedly to give them greater access to services; however, these services have failed to materialize. Although the TPLF/EPRDF[18] regime claims there is no connection between these forced evictions and

---

18 Meles Zenawi belonged to the Tigrayan People's Liberation Front (TPLF), which was the main constituent of the Ethiopian People's Revolutionary Democratic Front (EPRDF).

the government's new 'villagization projects;' recently released contracts between the government and these investors promise to provide 'vacant land free of any impediments,' which appears to mean those currently living on the land.

There were irregularities galore with the way the deals had been reached, and were ominous too:

The lack of transparency in these deals is clearly calculated; particularly in light of the 18 February 2010 report from the Financial Action Task Force (FATF) that found Ethiopia to be one of the five most at risk countries in the world for money laundering (AML) and the financing of terrorism (CFT);[19] stating that the lack of such compliance made not only Ethiopia, but also others involved with them, whether inside or outside their borders, extremely vulnerable to illicit activities.

The bottomline was simple: foreign companies were willy-nilly colluding with a repressive and corrupt regime in driving away Ethiopian farmers and pastoralists out of their ancestral lands. The story was out, but did not hit the headlines in India even though the name of an Indian company kept surfacing repeatedly through the litany of unending Ethiopian woes. It disappeared without a whimper into the proverbial news hole—though routine stories kept appearing intermittently.

All this while Bengaluru-based freelance journalist Keya Acharya had been observing the developments from a distance. Acharya had seen Karuturi's farms some years earlier in Karnataka, as also the company's rose farms at Naivasha, Kenya. She had not

---

19 Anti-money laundering (AML) is a term used in financial and legal circles to describe the legal controls that require financial institutions and other regulated entities to prevent, detect, and report money laundering activities. CFT is combating of the financing of terrorism. The two terms are often used together.

ventured into the Naivasha farms; only driven round from the outside. 'I had also reported, way back in 2007, about Karuturi being the largest dealer in cut-roses in the world. As background to that story, I had read a fellow journalist, Ochieng Ogodo's report in the *Guardian* about the environmental problems caused to Lake Naivasha from leachates and pesticides from Karuturi's farms adjoining the lake. The managing director of Karuturi Global, Sai Ramkrishna Karuturi had in the story told me, when I met him, that he had taken all precautions to prevent pollution of the lake, that he was very mindful of labour welfare measures, etc. Besides, having lived for many years in East Africa myself, I was familiar with Kenya and the region in question; so I had a basic background knowledge of the socio-cultural circumstances surrounding my story,' Acharya said.

In 2014, she decided on work on a story on the state of India's cut-rose sector for the international news and features agency Inter-Press Service (IPS). 'The reason I went for this story was that I found that recent reports, all negative, about Karuturi and his rose farms, was in sharp contrast to Karuturi Global's earlier image of being the best rose industry unit in the world. There were reports of poor management, non-payment of wages, alleged land-grab in Ethiopia, crop failures, collapsing firms, etc,' she told the authors of this book.

Acharya wanted to find out what led to this decline and to see what it had done to the rose industry in general in the region (Kenya and Ethiopia), run mostly by Indian companies. 'But since I was unable to contact Karuturi, in spite of repeated phone calls to his office, my story became one where other Indian cut-rose manufacturers discussed their issues in the backdrop of the negativity surrounding a fellow Indian concern that was now awash with negative reports.'

The story, 'India's Cut-Rose Sector Pushes Past Barriers', appeared online on 18 July 2014. It was a typical business story, with the impact of Karuturi Global's business practices and track record taking up roughly a fourth of the story length. A fortnight later the rose major retaliated. The reaction came in the form of a legal notice sent to Acharya by a legal firm called Pastay Law. The notice, also sent to IPS and two other businessmen quoted in the story saying that Karuturi's track record had had a negative bearing on India's cut-rose exports, alleged that the report had been a mud-slinging endeavour, and a conspiracy too. It claimed that Karuturi and his family members had to face embarrassing situations because of the report.

The nine-page notice ended with Karuturi's lawyers asking for, among other things, an unconditional apology, and asking Acharya to pay ₹50 crore damages for causing a loss of reputation and another ₹50 crore for causing mental agony to the client and his family members.

The two businessmen quoted were rivals of Karuturi, who was squarely blamed for the withering state of rose affairs:

> According to a disgruntled rose-grower and former chief of the forest services in the neighbouring state of Andhra Pradesh, RD Reddy, Ramakrishna [Karuturi] is 'a playboy in all respects; one who speculated in stocks with borrowed money and lost heavily, and now the whole industry in India is being blamed because of him.'

> Dr Manjunatha Reddy, a Dubai-based Indian industrialist with a rose farm located just five km away from Karuturi's flower operations in the Holata region, near the Ethiopian capital Addis Ababa, says that the 'takeover on paper' in the Gambella region is symptomatic of Ramakrishna's speculative Ponzi-like financial schemes.

'His misdeeds have really turned public sentiment against Indian industry in Africa,' he told IPS, adding that a bad commercial reputation goes viral in a continent where local communities rely heavily on the land for their livelihoods.

Reddy says other Indian enterprises like telecommunications and farming have also been tarnished with the same negative image cast by Karuturi's actions on the ground.

'We now have difficulty even in raising funds for agri-business from venture capitalists and investment brokers,' Reddy asserted.

Karuturi's head offices in Bangalore did not respond to IPS' repeated requests for an interview.

IPS went down on its knees immediately. It did something that major and well-known media houses and news agencies, in spite of their innumerable faults, are not quite reputed to do—it yanked off the story from its website, and left Acharya to fend for herself. It did not stand either by the report or its reporter. The notice itself had caught the journalist off-guard: 'I wasn't prepared in the least for legal action. I couldn't understand at first what it was that bothered the man so much to send me a ₹100 crore defamation notice. In fact, much of my bemusement still stands: there is nothing at all (apart from the quotes from people in the story) that is already not recorded or written.'

Acharya was right. Almost all she had mentioned in the story had already been in the public domain, and there had been innumerable negative stories about the company since the 2011 *Guardian*/IRIN reports.

In fact, in February 2013, Ethiopian activists had landed up on Indian shores to make a public cause of the plight of farmers and pastoralists. The Oakland Institute, in partnership with Indian civil society groups Indian Social Action Forum (INSAF), Kalpavriksh, and Centre for Social Development (CSD) organised an event in New Delhi where the issues were raised and a briefing paper titled 'India's land acquisition in Ethiopia: Benefactor or Colonizer?' was circulated. There was ample reason for Ethiopians to address the Indian media. Between 2008 and 2011, Ethiopia had leased out nearly 3.6 million hectares of land for commercial farm ventures to domestic and foreign investors. Most of these investments were made possible by the Ethiopian government's 'villagization programme' that would forcibly relocate over 1.5 million people from their homes. With over 600,000 hectares of land already acquired at that stage and several agro-industrial projects under way, Indian enterprises comprised the largest share of investors in that country. Between 2006 and 2009, Indian companies invested $4 billion in Ethiopian farmland. This was an Indian story too, but hardly made news in this country.

Facts were laid out threadbare. The Indian government did not have a direct role to play in the Ethiopian land-grab scam, but the public sector Export-Import Bank of India (EXIM Bank) had already opened a $640 million line of credit to the Ethiopian government to expand the country's sugar sector. This credit line required Ethiopia to import 75 per cent of the project goods and services, such as consultancy services, from India. Moreover, the apex association representing big business interests, the Federation of Indian Chambers of Commerce and Industry (FICCI) had been championing the overall investment activity there. There were stories here and there, but nothing to set the mediascape on fire.

Even earlier, in 2012, New York-headquartered Human Rights Watch (HRW) had specifically flayed Karuturi Global in its report *Waiting Here for Death: Forced Displacement and Villagization in Ethiopia's Gambella Region*, which had detailed the involuntary nature of the transfers, the loss of livelihoods, the deteriorating food situation, and ongoing abuses by the armed forces against the affected people. Some newspapers did carry news items on the HRW findings, and also courteously included flat denials of the accusations by the company.

The human rights organisation underscored:

> In a response to questions sent by Human Rights Watch, Karuturi stated that the company 'has not caused in any manner, any displacement of human habitation in order to make way forward for the project and is living in peaceful harmony with the people of Gambella.' However, Human Rights Watch's visit to the Karuturi lease area in May 2011 found that Anuak maize, sorghum, and groundnut crops had been cleared without consent. Some residents moved as a result.

All through, Karuturi's line of defence had been that it was playing by the rules set by the Ethiopian government. That, incidentally, was also the word coming from official sources in New Delhi. 'Land is a very sensitive issue. If it was done forcefully people wouldn't have let that happen. Most of these voices are those of overseas Ethiopians, many of whom were not in agreement with the policies of Zenawi, who they felt was an autocrat,' Indian officials told the *Hindu* newspaper. The Manmohan Singh government, under fire from all quarters for either indulging in or abetting land-grabbing across the country, was unlikely to take a stand in favour of the farmers or pastoralists in faraway Ethiopia. By conniving at the deeds of Ethiopian strongman Zenawi, who died in August 2012 after contracting an infection in Belgium, the Indian government had precisely not done what the Oakland Institute had urged it to during the February 2013 Delhi event:

> Foreign states, like the Indian government, also have extraterritorial human rights obligations vis-à-vis the Ethiopian populace. The

Maastricht Principles[20] lay out guidelines to ensure at minimum that governments do not create—or permit their own domestic actors to create—adverse human rights effects in foreign countries. In fact, under the Maastricht Principles, states are expected more comprehensively to respect, protect and fulfill the human rights of those residing in other states.

The dire situation of many indigenous communities in Ethiopia under the ongoing villagization program should trigger serious concerns under the Maastricht Principles for foreign governments that host corporate investors with a hand in Ethiopian land deals.

By the time Acharya wrote the article for IPS, the tide had started turning against Karuturi Global. In fact, the going got rough shortly after the first series of reports of land-grabbing in 2011, not only for Karuturi Global, but also other Indian companies. The *Hindu*, probably the only Indian newspaper with a correspondent stationed in Africa, reported in October 2012 of Indian companies 'which invested in controversial deals involving hundreds of thousands of acres of land in Ethiopia have found themselves out of their depth in a fast-growing African economy that is still in the process of building critical transport and irrigation networks.'

Karuturi Global had its share of unforeseen problems. A river that flowed through its 100,000 hectare farmland in Gambella breached a series of dykes in August 2011 and inundated vast tracts

---

20 The Maastricht Principles on Extraterritorial Obligations of States in the area of Economic, Social and Cultural Rights were adopted on 28 September 2011 by leading experts in international law and human rights at a meeting organised by Maastricht University and the International Commission of Jurists. The Maastricht Principles clarify the human rights obligations of States beyond their own borders, especially their obligation to avoid causing harm and to protect human rights extraterritorially. The Maastricht Principles filled a critical gap in the international legal framework, allowing governments to effectively respond to the negative impacts of globalisation that cannot be addressed or regulated by one State alone.

of its own farm, besides many villages. The widespread allegation against the company was that it had altered the natural course of the river with the dykes, which resulted in the deluge that caused villagers to be displaced. At that time, according to the *Hindu*, the company was 'saddled with ₹753 crore of debt and re-scheduled a $55 million foreign currency bond at a time when global financial markets have tightened and European flower demand has contracted.' The scenario was getting less rosy, and more thorny for Karuturi. Till June 2013, it had been able to develop only 5 per cent of the land area that it had been allotted.

Over time, Karuturi Global began losing ground as public campaigns and movements gathered momentum in that country. And, if the post-Zenawi Ethiopian government's decision to review its policy of leasing out land to investors was not bad enough news, worse was to come from the US Congress in the form of the 2014 Omnibus Appropriations Bill which contained provisions that ensured that US development funds were not used to support forced evictions in Ethiopia. The Oakland Institute assessed the bill thus:

> The bill prevents US assistance from being used to support activities that directly or indirectly involve forced displacement in the Lower Omo and Gambella regions. It further requires US assistance in these areas be used to support local community initiatives aimed at improving livelihoods and be subject to prior consultation with affected populations. The bill goes further and even instructs the directors of international financial institutions to oppose financing for any activities that directly or indirectly involve forced evictions in Ethiopia.

The Ethiopian measures that promoted crony capitalism and accentuated human rights abuses were increasingly finding fewer takers. And Karuturi Global's dwindling fortunes overlapped with

these developments. Its share prices had dropped from a high of
₹42.70 on 9 January 2008 to ₹3.24 exactly five years later at the
Bombay Stock Exchange (BSE). Its total income from operations
fell from ₹38.25 crore in March 2008 to ₹19.15 crore during the
same period. Ramkrishna Karuturi, the managing director of his
eponymous Karuturi Global, was hardly anymore the golden boy
of 2008. Acharya's report, therefore, had nothing sensational or
new to reveal about Karuturi Global.

Till this point, most of whatever had appeared in the media about
Karuturi Global's unholy liaison with the Ethiopian government
had been glossed over by the Indian news establishment, or
those had been outright business stories about the growth of
the company or the constraints that it was facing. But Acharya's
story was for IPS, a global news agency. 'It was not written with
an Indian readership in mind, but with the global perspective of
seeing what the Indian rose industry both here in India and in the
countries in question, felt about what had impacted them from
(Ramkrishna) Karuturi's image.'

The legal notice, therefore, was a bolt from the blue. 'I had, at
first, thought it was a 'fake notice' just to intimidate me, since the
notice had no proper letterhead of the legal office from where it
emanated on Karuturi Global's behalf; it had no proper signature
either. But legal reaction of my son (who is a lawyer) to the notice
made me tighten up. When the head of the legal media defence
organisation he put me in touch with looked at my case and said
that I needed a lawyer, I was seriously alert to my predicament,
and indignantly angry at the same time that the notice mentioned
withdrawal of the case if I issued a public, written apology. When
I told my defence lawyer that I would not apologise, he told me to
get ready to fight,' Acharya said. She was ready to take the fight
right into the 'enemy' camp.

But if Karuturi Global had often figured in negative stories and the company was only known for issuing routine denials and rhetoric assertions about the good work that it was doing in Africa, the legal attack on Acharya in that case defied both logic as well as bucked a trend. What was also true was that all the laudatory stories and wishy-washy interviews that had appeared in the Indian media had been during Karuturi's upswing days. At the time of the IPS article, which only figured Karuturi Global in the context of the cut-rose export market, the company was not only fighting with its back to the wall over its apparent non-performance in Ethiopia, it had also been pushed into a corner in neighbouring Kenya from where it had charted out its spectacular growth.

When Sai Ramakrishna Karuturi launched his operations in the Ethiopian capital of Addis Ababa, his company was already the world's largest producer of cut-roses. Yet, the founder and managing director of Karuturi Global wanted to move beyond what he had been doing for the past seven years in Kenya, floriculture. Karuturi had established his organisation in 1994, shortly after completing his engineering degree from Bangalore University. At that time, floriculture accounted for 95 per cent of the company's revenues and 99 per cent of its profits. It had a 10 per cent share of the European market for roses.

Karuturi Global's operations were perhaps too clean to be true. The first aspersions on its flowery image were cast in December 2010 when its stocks fell 10 per cent on reports that the Intelligence Bureau (IB) was investigating it for alleged insider trading. On 2 July 2013, market regulator Securities and Exchange Board of India (SEBI) slapped penalties worth ₹40 lakh on the promoters of Karuturi Global for alleged violations of various norms like requisite disclosure about shareholding patterns. In seven separate orders, SEBI imposed penalties on Ramakrishna Karuturi and the company's three promoter entities—Anitha Karuturi, Rhea Holdings and Simply Class Fashions—for violations of various regulations. Fines were also imposed on director Anil T and persons acting in concert with the company's promoters.

One order was a penalty of ₹3 lakh on Ramakrishna Karuturi alone for indulging in insider trading activities and not making requisite disclosure regarding his shareholding. SEBI found that he had traded in shares of the company while the trading window was closed. He ought to have taken permission from the company before trading, but he had failed to do so. Another order fined Ramakrishna Karuturi, three promoters and Anil T an amount of ₹15 lakh for failure to make a public announcement regarding acquisition of a substantial number of the company's shares. Anitha Karuturi and Simply Class Fashions were fined ₹2 lakh each, while Rhea Holdings was fined ₹3 lakh for not making requisite disclosures to the company and the stock exchange concerned. Suddenly, Ramakrishna Karuturi was not that golden boy anymore.

The SEBI scandal came in the wake of Karuturi figuring in the list of 612 Indians exposed in one of the biggest global investigations on tax evasion carried out by the International Consortium of Investigative Journalists (ICIJ) in May 2014. The ICIJ had collaborated with several media organisations around the world, collected 260 gigabytes of data and about 2.5 million files, and included investigation by 68 journalists from 46 countries, thereby exposing the secret world of more than 120,000 offshore companies. The *Indian Express*, which was the ICIJ's Indian partner in the Offshore Leaks investigations, reported:

> The world's largest producer of cut roses, Sai Ramakrishna
> Karuturi, also appears in the documents. He and his wife

Anitha appear to have registered six BVI (British Virgin Islands) companies in 2007. Reached in Ethiopia he said he did not recall setting up any offshore companies and he did not respond to follow-up calls.

But neither the SEBI-related misdemeanours nor the reports of offshore accounts had been mentioned in Acharya's story. In fact, IPS had in November 2011 carried an Addis-Ababa-datelined story which had specifically looked at Ethiopian land-grabbing allegations. Even this report had mentioned only one company: Karuturi Global. The report started off with the plight of farmers:

> Kneeling in the middle of a sugar cane field in blistering 40 degree heat, a young boy is digging up weeds while an Indian worker stands over him to make sure he does not miss any. Red is eight years old and earns 73 pence for one day's work—less than the cost of using pesticides.

> By exporting food produced by child labour in Ethiopia, an Indian farm manager hopes to earn millions within three years. 'It's still total wilderness here, but we will soon start growing sugar cane and palm oil and everything will look tidy,' explains Karmjeet Singh Sekhon as he drives in a Toyota 4x4 through the burning bushland on his farm.

> The 68-year-old Indian is the manager of a huge farm, which covers an area of 100,000 hectares in Western Ethiopia. Soon he wants to farm 300,000 hectares, an area bigger than Luxembourg.

It made no bones about how Karuturi Global was out there only to make money:

> It is not surprising that the Ethiopian government has become the darling of international agribusiness investors. 'There is plenty

of good land, enough water, a cheap labour force, and a stable
government that ensures law and order,' says Karuturi's Singh
[Sekhon].

...

According to the government, there is no link between the relocation
and the farm projects; everybody moves voluntarily. Human right
groups doubt this, and the author was obstructed several times
during the research for this article. The official reason given was:
'We don't want you to gather politically unwanted information.'

As well as human rights organisations, environmentalists also
have a problem with the farms. Some four decades ago, 40 per
cent of Ethiopia was covered by forest, but today it is less than
three per cent—and the bushland in Gambella is burning.

Farm manager Sekhon does not hide his lack of interest in
environmental concerns. For him, it is important to develop the
farm, and he is behind his ambitious schedule. To catch up, little
Red and his friends must continue weeding.

The 2014 IPS article by Acharya, in many ways, went beyond both
her 2007 piece about the state of India's cut-rose market as well
as the agency's 2011 report about land-grabbing. Every allegation
about Karuturi Global had either been religiously reported or
done to death. *Business Standard* newspaper alone had carried a
number of articles and reports about its activities. In January 2012,
its columnist Sreelatha Menon wrote that even though 'Karuturi
claims it is clean, the goings-on in that country are far from it.'

The financial troubles were diligently reported as well (in
August 2013):

Analysts and investors, in addition to the weakness in the
operations and debt, are concerned about the drastic drop in

promoter shareholding in the company as lenders are aggressively invoking pledges. The company, which has under lease expansive tracts spanning about 3,00,000 hectares, has been at the centre of a controversy over alleged land grabbing as well.

In the recent past, credit-rating agency ICRA [formerly Investment Information and Credit Rating Agency of India Limited, or IICRA India] had flagged concerns, stating there were risks associated with the foray into agriculture. The risks included execution and logistical ones, which could be compounded by adverse climatic changes, resulting in lower-than-expected yields of agricultural and floricultural products.

And then, there was the Kenyan angle too. Karuturi Global had expanded there by acquiring Kenya-based Sher Agencies (later renamed Sher Karuturi) in September 2007 from Dutch horticulturists Gerrit & Peter Barnhoorn. This acquisition brought into its fold a 188-hectare farmland in the Naivasha region. If Karuturi Global was being accused of driving off farmers and pastoralists from their homelands in Ethiopia, in the neighbouring country it was charged with steamrolling workers. The *Business Standard* wrote:

Karuturi Global, the Bangalore-based publicly-held rose exporter, has recently seen the troubles with its employees in Kenya escalating over a wage settlement. This has snowballed into a winding-up petition filed by a packaging company which is part of the Aga Khan Development Network.[21] Karuturi Global, which rose dramatically on to the global stage as among the leading rose exporters to Europe from Africa, is already in various stages

---

21 The Aga Khan Development Network (AKDN) is a network of private, non-denominational development agencies established to improve the quality of life of 'the Ismailis and the broader societies in which they live' particularly in the sub-Saharan Africa, Central and South Asia, and the Middle East.

of untangling issues over its ambitious agriculture foray in Ethiopia, which is facing backlash and is in the midst of various problems.

According to Karuturi Global, it is facing a winding-up petition from Allpack Industries and discussions are in the preliminary stages. According to recent reports, as a result of the financial troubles which Karuturi Global is under, it has not been able to pay salaries to employees at its expansive rose farms.

There were the, now-usual, denials:

However, Karuturi has refuted the charges stating that Kenya Planters and Agricultural Workers Union officials have advised their members to reject the salaries for August and September 2013, and instead engage in various violent demonstrations pending the hearing and determination of various suits filed in the industrial court in Nakuru.

Kenya's *Daily Nation* described Karuturi Global as a thorn among roses:

After ruling the flower industry roost for years, rose producer, Karuturi, is broke. A blue chip company touted as the world's cut flower giant, then known Sher Agencies, the enterprise was a darling of job seekers.

But the story is no-longer rosy after its ownership changed hands in 2008 becoming Karuturi. It is now debt-laden and employees who have gone unpaid for months are striking.

Its debts run into billions of [Kenyan] shillings. [Its] Indian-based Bangalore subsidiary owes at least Sh400 million to CFC Stanbic Bank and other creditors, while the Kenya Revenue Authority is demanding Sh962 million in alleged tax evasion after the firm was found guilty of transfer mispricing.

Even as Acharya was scripting her legal response to Karuturi Global, international non-profit GRAIN which works with small farmers and social movements in their struggles for community-controlled and biodiversity-based food systems, issued a statement saying that its 'flower trading subsidiary in the Netherlands had been declared bankrupt, while a Dutch industry source reported that one of its farms in Ethiopia had been sold off to a company in Dubai.'

GRAIN, which like the Oakland Institute, had been tracking Karuturi, provided the backdrop:

> Meanwhile, the company was on the hook for millions of dollars in unpaid taxes and debts. In 2012, the Kenya Revenue Authority determined that Karuturi, which had once been producing close to a million roses a year at its Naivasha farm for an eager European market, failed to pay $20 million worth of taxes due to transfer mispricing.

> In 2013, the company was taken to court in Kenya for failure to pay its creditors. Unpaid workers went on strike, the Karuturi Hospital suffered power cuts, and free schooling for the flower farmworkers' children at Karuturi School came to an end. The community around the farm in Naivasha continues to bear the economic and social costs of the Indian company's troubles.

> In early 2014, the Kenyan courts finally determined that Karuturi Ltd was bankrupt and put the flower farm in receivership, despite protests from Karuturi.

So, if all that Karuturi Global and Ramakrishna Karuturi had found to be defamatory in Acharya's report had already been written about or reported on many times over, why did they gun for her?

At the time of the Acharya article, Ramakrishna Karuturi was trying to regain his farms in Kenya, restart his agricultural farms in Ethiopia, and trying to wriggle out of the SEBI quagmire. Karuturi might have wanted to use this legal notice against IPS and the reporter to ward off any adverse reporting on him and his operations in Kenya and Ethiopia. Moreover, IPS was not an Indian publication and Acharya was an independent journalist without any publishing house support in India. This suspicion is borne out of the fact that a number of adverse reports about Karuturi Global appeared in the Indian media even after the publication of the IPS one, but neither Karuturi nor his company reacted to any of them. There is a fallacy here, for a person can choose who to have been offended or defamed by, and who to send a legal notice to.

The legal notice did leave an impression on Acharya. 'The agency (Inter-Press Service) that carried this article was one where I had been a correspondent for about 15 years (since 1999). That they folded like a pack of cards and offered me absolutely no support was distressing for me. It led to an immediate cessation of my wanting to do anything more with the agency. At this seniority, freelancing again, as opposed to being an independent, regular correspondent for a news agency where my work for them won me two awards and positive recognition for them, was not an easy prospect,' she rued. Acharya, who had co-edited *The Green Pen: Environmental Journalism in India and the South Asian Region* with fellow journalist Frederick Noronha in 2010, won the Prem Bhatia Award for Excellence in Environmental Reporting in 2008, and was presented with the Green Globe Award for Outstanding Contribution by a Mediaperson two years later.

Being let down by one's own publication is the worst thing that can happen to a journalist. So, did Acharya regret having done the cut-rose story? 'I had no second thoughts on writing the story, though I will admit I did have some instinct at the back of my mind about two of the adjectives that the IPS editorial had added (one called him 'notorious', and though I now have a whole dossier of writing and evidence to support that adjective, it's not a description I would have normally added). The story had already come back to me twice before that, and I had, in writing, expressed my dismay at the quality of the editing,' she remarked on her interaction with IPS.

On 17 July 2014, she wrote to IPS Asia Editor Kanya d'Almeida, 'There are several areas that have inaccurate nuances in the story that you've sent back. I've corrected the major assumptions in point form right at the beginning of the attached story. I'm a little fazed by the amount of re-phrasing that's been done to the story. It's both unsettling and 'new' for me, considering I've been writing for IPS for decades now. Perhaps if you gave me a writing guide the next time, I'd understand what exactly you're wanting?' So when the story came back to her for the third time, 'again with words and phrases put into it, I sort of let it go. Be that as it may, there was still nothing in the story to warrant the charges that were put on me.' The story was released the following day.

Karuturi's own troubles were, however, far from over. Addis Ababa-based portal *TheReporter* updated the company's continuing Ethiopian travails on 17 January 2015:

> Karuturi Global, which earlier agreed with the ministry of agriculture (MoA) to grow wheat on 300 thousand hectares of fertile land has fell [sic] to deliver its promises of becoming a leading agricultural company.

> Karuturi was almost foreclosed after failing to repay a 65 million birr (a little over $3 million) loan extended via overdraft facility from the state-owned Commercial Bank of Ethiopia (CBE). However, the company immediately settled the minimum 25 per cent of the debt. But government officials told *TheReporter* that Karuturi is no longer reputed in Ethiopia.

Abera Mulat, director of agricultural investment and land administration agency, at the MoA told *TheReporter* that Karuturi [is] no longer a reputable company in Ethiopia. According to Abera, the Indian giant has failed to deliver. The official went on to say that Karuturi is on the verge of collapsing in Ethiopia. 'Karuturi has gone bankrupt following internal management crisis,' Abera said.

In July 2015, Group CEO and CFO Shireesh Jain resigned. Karuturi Global stated in a filing with the Bombay Stock Exchange (BSE), 'Shireesh Jain, Chief Executive Officer (CEO) and Chief Financial Officer (CFO) is no longer working for the company. He is no longer associated with the affairs of the company.' The board had accepted his resignation, the company said without disclosing reasons.

Karuturi Global was far from being out of the woods, but the defamation notice against Keya Acharya was a case study in itself. For, here was a company nothing like Reliance Industries, Sahara India Pariwar or Essar in size, and yet was sending a defamatory notice and asking for as much in damages. On the other hand, the hounding of Acharya was that of harassing a freelance journalist where the publisher of the so-called defamatory article had left its own correspondent high and dry.

Almost as a *fait accompli*, Acharya stopped writing for IPS, something that she had been doing for 15 long years, but the one issue that cropped up during the parting of ways could happen to any journalist, especially freelancers. She explained, 'There is one other point in this whole scenario—one that concerns the media itself. And that is the question of what publications/publishing houses should be doing. In my case, a large, global news agency that touts itself as a champion of human rights and fights for the downtrodden, using freelance journalists from around the world, including those reporting from dangerous, conflict zones, folded like a pack of cards in fright at the notice and left one of its senior freelance correspondents to fend for herself, in spite of definite editorial responsibility.'

Acharya did send a befitting reply to Karuturi Global backing each assertion in the story with web links to news items which backed up the allegations (and were all in the public domain). In the year between the legal response and the writing of this book, Karuturi Global's fortunes had dwindled considerably. The rosy picture of 2007 had long faded away; all that it could do was send a defamation to an independent journalist, while at the same time sending supplicatory responses to big newspapers that kept publishing negative stories about Karuturi Global and its founder.

Not particularly brave, one would say.

5

Money over Matter

The Global Financial Crisis (GFC) of 2008 and its worldwide impact had set analysts and economists introspecting. There were many who attracted criticism for the economic disaster, and among them were financial journalists. The financial press was incessantly and mercilessly castigated in the West for not providing any forewarning to the general public, for lacking sufficient scepticism when thoughtlessly reporting on financial and economic trends, and for its reporters being perceived to be too close to the sources they used for information. Three Australian researchers in July 2015 published a quantitative and qualitative content analysis of the reportage in three mainstream newspapers in the United States, the United Kingdom, and Australia across three decades, along with industry insights provided by interviews with reporters in each of the countries studied.

The study of Sophie Knowles, Gail Phillips and Johan Lidberg, *Reporting the Global Financial Crisis: A Longitudinal Tri-nation Study of Mainstream Financial Journalism*, found that the GFC represented only the 'latest manifestation of dissatisfaction with the financial press, with similar concerns being raised in previous financial crises such as the recession of the late 1990s and the Dot

Com Boom in 2000.' The researchers from Monash University concluded:

Since the global recession of 1990, financial reporting in three reputable mainstream publications has been increasingly limited in the range of interpretations and versions of events, has relied on a narrowing range of sources, and has focused its attention on investor issues often at the expense of a broader scrutiny of the financial system and economic developments. The content analysis confirms arguments found in the literature:

1. There is a diminishing number of warnings and a general lack of scepticism to alert the public to dangers.

2. There is a narrowing range of sources that certainly does exclude the 'average person.'

3. There is a reliance on overarching narratives and official sources, including public relations and those who are directly implicated in the crisis, to define events at a crucial point in the crises' development.

The crisis was that of financial journalism too. The sum and substance of the study was this: financial journalists had a critical role to play in economic stability, and therefore during crises too.

Back home in India, as businesses grew and the economy did too, more attention was paid to financial markets. Financial market journalism gradually became a niche within business journalism. This was a demanding expertise—a journalist would have to keep both a hawk's eye on developments in a fluid situation, as well as maintain one's own credibility so as not to play into the hands of vested interests. The key to reporting on financial markets was knowing how things worked and money flowed. One such journalist in India was Mumbai-based Sucheta Dalal. On 23 April 1992, Dalal exposed stockbroker Harshad Mehta's illegal methods through articles in the *Times of India*. Mehta was dipping illegally into the banking system to finance his own buying. What Mehta and his associates did was siphon off funds from inter-bank transactions and buy shares heavily at a premium across many segments, thereby triggering off a rise in the sensitive index of the Bombay Stock Exchange (BSE).

Dalal wrote of what came to be known as the Securities Scam:

> The crucial mechanism through which the scam was effected was the ready forward (RF) deal. The RF is in essence a secured short-term (typically 15-day) loan from one bank to another. Crudely put, the bank lends against government securities just as a pawnbroker lends against jewellery. The borrowing bank actually sells the securities to the lending bank and buys them back at the end of the period of the loan, typically at a slightly higher price. It was this ready forward deal that Mehta and his accomplices used with great success to channel money from the banking system.

Mehta had figured out an ingenious way to dupe the system. But as his luck would have it, so had Dalal. She went on to co-author a book on the scam with husband Debashis Basu titled *The Scam: Who Won, Who Lost, Who Got Away* (1993). It was revised and re-released in 2001 and again in 2005 under the new title *The Scam: From Harshad Mehta to Ketan Parekh*. In March 2006, she launched *MoneyLife*, a fortnightly personal finance magazine, a business news website (moneylife.in) and a non-profit registered trust—Moneylife Foundation—to promote financial literacy and consumer and investor initiatives. She continued her watchdog role, undeterred and with utmost intensity.

The report of Dalal that would alter the course of the very debate about defamation and critical reportage was to come much later. On 14 January 2015, a whistle-blower claiming to be based out of Singapore and working for a hedge fund wrote a letter to BK

Gupta, a deputy general manager (DGM) at market regulator SEBI (Securities and Exchange Board of India) alleging massive technical manipulation at the National Stock Exchange (NSE). The letter, which was also marked to Dalal, alleged that the manipulation was allowing some players to wield unfair advantage over others. The eight-page letter elaborated on the technical details of the game, most of which would be mumbo jumbo to the uninitiated.

For the next five months, Dalal tried to verify the allegations. *MoneyLife* wrote to the SEBI chairman, NSE chairman Ravi Narain, and NSE managing director Chitra Ramakrishnan, asking whether they had acted on the document, but evoked no response. The letter was also shared with exchanges, regulators, government agencies and key traders. Finally, Dalal concluded that the only people who could throw light on it 'are actual HFT (high-frequency trading) players who understand how this game is played.'

On 19 June 2015, *MoneyLife* put up the document on its website to crowd-source opinion and facts. It contended that the subject at hand was crucial:

> High-frequency trading using colocation[22] that give traders advantages by a few milliseconds have come to occupy the centrestage of equity markets all over the world. Such automated trading, which executes pre-programmed instructions, generating thousands to millions of trades every trading day come out of black boxes designed by whiz kids in the secret corners of trading firms. If deployed unfairly, a tiny unfair advantage can translate into crores of rupees of illegal profit.

> *MoneyLife* has repeatedly argued that India has no system of monitoring complex automated systems, leave along trading

---

22 A colocation centre is a data centre where equipment, space, and bandwidth are available for rental to retail customers.

transactions. Consequently, organisations that operate such technology have become a law unto themselves, supervised by nobody. Even when there is a major glitch or a fat finger trade, no report is put into the public domain.

The concerns were almost echoed by the Reserve Bank of India (RBI) in its Financial Stability Report (FSR) for June 2015 that was released six days later:

> The concerns emanating from rapid rise in algorithmic and high frequency trading in recent years highlight the need for caution for India's securities markets, even as significant steps have been taken with regard to move towards risk based supervision, preventing and dealing with illegal money-raising activities and insider trading.

It also spoke of 'the increased complexities of algorithm coding and reduction in latency due to faster communication platforms needs focused monitoring as they may pose risks in the form of increased possibilities of error trades and market manipulation.

Algo trading refers to the use of electronic platforms for entering trading orders with a computer programme (called algorithm) determining the decisions on aspects such as the timing, price, or quantity of the order or in many cases initiating the order without human intervention. HFT is a special class of algo trading, in which computers make elaborate decisions to initiate orders based on electronically accessed information at a very fast speed (in microseconds), before human traders are capable of processing the information they observe.

On 21 July, the NSE responded to *MoneyLife*. A terse press release cut the story short:

> NSE has filed a defamation suit today, against an organization and its representatives who published unsubstantiated and misleading

reports against the exchange. The exchange has sought withdrawal of those reports etc, as well as, has made a claim of ₹100 crore (which can be revised upwards). These reports referred to algo trading mechanism etc.

As you know since inception, NSE has been maintaining a high degree of surveillance and integrity in its day to day operation, strictly adheres to the rules, regulations and guidelines issued by the regulators from time to time.

The matter is now pending in the hon'ble High Court of Mumbai.

The NSE's assertions, however, were thrown out of the window by the high court on 9 September 2015. The court said the NSE's refusal to answer repeated queries from Dalal prior to publication of the articles in question, either amounted to arrogance or meant there was truth in the allegations put forth. It dismissed the case, and ordered the NSE to pay ₹1.5 lakh each to Dalal and Basu and another ₹47 lakh as punitive damages to the Tata Memorial and Masina Hospitals in Mumbai (to be paid in the form of donation). It was a landmark judgment.

The order of a single-judge bench comprising Justice GS Patel, not only looked into the technical issues involved in its judgment, it also made telling comments on defamation, free speech and intimidation. The biggest take was that the NSE was not allowed to get away with its browbeating tactics.

Justice Patel came down heavily on the NSE's inability to digest criticism:

I do not believe that a defamation action should be allowed to be used to negate or stifle genuine criticism, even pointed criticism or criticism that is harshly worded; nor should it be allowed to choke a fair warning to the public if its interest stands threatened in some way. It is to me a matter of very great dismay that the NSE should have attempted this action at all. Except where it is shown that the article complained of is facially defamatory, that is to say, it is *prima facie* intended to defame or libel, an injunction will not readily be granted. Every criticism is not defamation. Every person criticized is not defamed.

And the NSE would have to earn its respect, not tear it out of the throats of public it is meant to serve:

> The NSE is after all a public institution and it is in some sense or the other a custodian if not of public funds then at least of an undeniable public trust. This demands, I think, the most complete transparency, accountability and openness in its actions, dealing and operations. I include in this its duty to respond in a measured fashion to a question that has been placed in a measured fashion. It has no duty to respond to a wild or reckless allegation. But when a person, having made some enquiries, and herself having something of an established track record, makes a politely worded and pointed enquiry, not to respond to it seems to me either to be an example of the most egregious hubris and arrogance or, alternatively, an admission that there is an element of truth in what was being said. There is no third alternative.

The NSE had possibly got carried away by the absence of accountability that it otherwise enjoyed. The stock exchange has been practically unaccountable ever since it was established in 1992. SEBI, on the other hand, is answerable to capital markets as well as the country's finance minister. Besides, while SEBI changes its chairman every three years, the NSE is the only public or quasi-public entity where the top management has remained the same for the past 25 years. The NSE is not open to Right to Information (RTI) queries either.

It was, therefore, all the more important for an investigative

journalist to write about goings-on at the stock exchange. Justice
Patel spoke of the gravity of such stories:

> The scams that beleaguered our exchanges in the past, and those
> that continue to occupy the time of this court have at least in part
> come to light because of persons like Ms Dalal and her fellow
> travellers. If regulatory agencies have been compelled to make
> changes, and if our own Supreme Court has felt it necessary to
> step in with drastic orders, it is because every oversight process
> has either failed or been subverted. The plaintiffs are in error
> when they describe Ms Dalal as some out-of-control lone wolf.
> The nation may or may not want to know; Ms Dalal does. So do
> her readers. And, as it happens, so do I. She is certainly entitled
> to ask, to question, to doubt and to draw legitimate conclusions.

Turning the NSE's allegation on its head, the court spoke on the
role of journalists:

> It is fashionable these days to deride every section of the media
> as mere paparazzi, chasing the salacious and steamy. We forget
> again. None of the scams and the leaks of the past two decades
> would have been possible without journalists, editors, newspapers
> and television news anchors. We have grown accustomed to
> mocking them. We deride their manner, describing them as loud,
> brash, obnoxious, abrasive and opinionated. We forget. We forget
> that but for them the many uncomfortable questions that must
> be asked of those in authority and those with the sheer muscle
> power of money would forever go unasked and unanswered. We
> forget that it is these persons we are so wont to mock who are,
> truly, the watchdogs of our body politic, the voice of our collective
> conscience, the sentinels on our ramparts. They may annoy. They
> may irritate. They certainly distress and cause discomfort. That
> is not only their job. It is their burden. Watchdogs respond to
> whistles and whistles need whistleblowers; and between them if

they can ask what others have not dared, if they can, if I may be permitted this, boldly go where none have gone before; if they can, as they say, rattle a few cages, then that is all to the good.

Justice Patel raised an important point in the judgment. He talked of the erstwhile 'Reynolds defence'[23] in English defamation law, which could be raised where it was clear that the journalist had a duty to publish an allegation even if it turned out to be wrong. In adjudicating on an attempted 'Reynolds defence', a court would investigate the conduct of the journalist and the content of the publication. [This provision was struck down in the Defamation Act of 2013.] The judge mentioned the ten criteria against which attempts to use the 'Reynolds defence' might be assessed, and felt that six of these echoed in the case in question.

The Bombay High Court judgment was an important one for

---

23   The Reynolds vs Times Newspapers Ltd case of 2001 provided the Reynolds Defence, which could be raised where it was clear that the journalist had a duty to publish an allegation even if it turned out to be wrong. The pointed ten codes to satisfy the responsible journalism in his judgment .They were

    1.   The seriousness of the allegation. The more serious the charge, the more the public is misinformed and the individual harmed, if the allegation is not true.

    2.   The nature of the information, and the extent to which the subject-matter is a matter of public concern.

    3.   The source of the information. Some informants have no direct knowledge of the events. Some have their own axes to grind, or are being paid for their stories.

    4.   The steps taken to verify the information.

    5.   The status of the information. The allegation may have already been the subject of an investigation which commands respect.

    6.   The urgency of the matter. News is often a perishable commodity.

    7.   Whether comment was sought from the plaintiff. He may have information others do not possess or have not disclosed. An approach to the plaintiff will not always be necessary.

    8.   Whether the article contained the gist of the plaintiff's side of the story.

    9.   The tone of the article. A newspaper can raise queries or call for an investigation. It need not adopt allegations as statements of fact.

  10. The circumstances of the publication, including the timing.

reporters, in setting a bar for journalistic standards as well as ethics, 'If there is indeed a factual error, can it be said to have been made in good faith, and in a reasonable belief that it was true? The 'actual malice' standard seems to me to suggest that one or both of these must be shown: intentional falsehood, or a reckless failure to attempt the verification that a reasonable person would. In this case, I do not think that the plaintiffs have met that standard, or demonstrated either intentional falsehood or a failure to attempt a verification. The burden of proof in claiming the qualified privilege that attaches to fair comment can safely be said to have been discharged.'

In simple words, Dalal and *MoneyLife* had done their duty, dutifully and diligently. More important, the judgment ought to serve as a word of caution for those wanting to browbeat journalists into submission: 'Today, all our institutions face the crisis of dwindling public confidence. Neither the NSE nor the judiciary are exceptions to this. It presents a very real dilemma, for the existence of our institutions is posited on that very public confidence and faith and its continuance. The challenge is, I think, in finding legitimate methods of restoring that public trust, that balance. Hence the cries for transparency and accountability everywhere; and I see no reason why the NSE should be any exception to this. Quelling dissent and doubt by strong-arming seems to me a decidedly odd way of going about restoring that public faith.'

Whether other courts of law would emulate Justice Patel's standards would be for them to decide, but what was clear for journalists was that the Bombay High Court had set precedents, formative ones at that.

Dalal and Basu's tribulations owing to the litigation did not last long. One could say they were relatively lucky—from the time of filing of the case to it being disposed of, it had been a matter of less than two months.

The hounding of Nitin Mangal, an equity research analyst who co-authored a scathing report, by the aggrieved Indiabulls conglomerate was, however, writ in harassment.

Equity research firms in India started gaining currency and credibility ever since Kawaljeet Saluja, an analyst at Kotak Securities, nosedived into the affairs of Satyam Computers by questioning why the company was keeping $550 million in current accounts. That was in October 2008. Among research firms that gradually started operations in India was the Canadian organisation, Veritas Investment Research. It started offering paid equity research on publicly traded Indian companies from 1 January 2012 and there was considerable interest in the so-called India Research Services. Mangal joined the firm as an analyst. The Veritas reports on Kingfisher Airlines in September 2011 and DLF in March 2012 had created quite a flutter in the market.

On 1 August 2012, in a report titled *Bilking India*[24] that was authored by senior analyst Neeraj Monga and Mangal, Veritas alleged that the Indiabulls management had thrown corporate governance to the winds so as to enrich a select group of shareholders. The report ran into 24 pages and included an additional 80 pages of supporting documents. 'We believe that disclosures at Indiabulls Real Estate Ltd (IBREL) and Indiabulls Power Ltd are unreliable and that the sole purpose of IBREL is to bilk institutional and retail investors for the benefit of select insiders. The controlling shareholders are running the organisation as a piggybank, while proclaiming propriety and espousing credibility.'

---

24 'Bilking' was originally a term used in the game of cards called cribbage, and denoted the spoiling of someone's score. Seventeenth century onwards, 'to bilk' clearly meant 'to defraud' someone.

The report, that was officially released exactly a week later, warned Indian financial institutions that lent to the group to 'watch out' and advised investors to 'sell all Indiabulls group stocks.' The market reaction was immediate, as stocks went into a tailspin. Indiabulls Real Estate fell as much as 17.3 per cent before recovering to be down 1.8 per cent. Indiabulls Financial Services went down 2.2 per cent, Indiabulls Power Ltd lost 4.4 per cent, while Indiabulls Securities dropped 3.3 per cent. In the month after, Indiabulls stock plummeted about 20 per cent, but thereafter the price rose by almost 100 per cent.

Indiabulls went after Veritas with all guns blazing. It issued full-page advertisements in newspapers giving its side of the story, and disputed the numbers and the analysis. 'The heavy bias for creating sensationalism for personal profiteering is the reason [for the report],' it said. Indiabulls Financial Services CEO Gagan Banga commented, 'The Veritas report is 100 per cent incorrect and fabricated... This is taking gullible investors for a ride by selectively leaking sensitive information, and then making money by selling such report. We have filed a criminal complaint against the agency as well as its author with the economic offences wing of the Mumbai Police presenting the facts in the case file.' Banga said nobody from Veritas had contacted the company, either before writing the report or before releasing it to the select brokers. 'Their *modus operandi* is to selectively leak the report and make money by selling it later. It's a brilliant (way) to hammer some stocks and make money out of that.'

In a detailed rebuttal of the points alleged in the report, Indiabulls argued, 'The allegations made are factually incorrect and have ignored disclosures in public domain made through the annual reports of FY11 and FY12,which have also been circulated to all shareholders.' The Veritas report said public disclosures made by Indiabulls Real Estate and Indiabulls Power were unreliable and the sole purpose of Indiabulls Real Estate 'is to bilk institutional and retail investors for the benefit of select insiders.'

Veritas claimed that it had analysed 57 group companies including private companies of controlling shareholders, 201 financial and legal documents including annual reports, annual returns, various schemes of arrangements filed in local courts, exchange filings, annexure details, etc, for the analysis. In different email statements to various Indian publications, Monga never denied that he hadn't ever met Indiabulls executives in the course of his research.

In a filing with the BSE, Indiabulls Real Estate said, 'Indiabulls officers filed a complaint with the police against the *mala fide* Veritas report along with email evidence where Neeraj Monga demanded money through his personal email and that if money was given in time he would hold back the report.' The police booked Monga, Mangal and Veritas under various sections in an FIR dated 8 August 2012. Indiabulls officials also initiated complaints with investigating agencies in Canada for causing harm and injury to the group and its shareholders. Monga was then the executive vice-president and head of global research at Veritas.

It took more than two years for the case to pick up speed. And when it did, it snowballed fast. Mangal was arrested by the police in Gurgaon, Haryana on 25 November 2014 on charges related to conspiracy, extortion and forgery of documents. It was reported that Monga, a resident of Vikaspuri in Delhi, had fled to Canada. The police said proceedings to get him declared a proclaimed offender would be initiated.

The battle was mostly fought in the courts. In August 2014, Veritas sued Indiabulls Real Estate Ltd and Indiabulls Housing Finance Ltd in Canada, claiming $10 million in general and special damages along with $1 million in punitive damages. Veritas, which had meanwhile shut down its India operations, alleged that the conduct of Indiabulls had caused 'irreparable damage to their business, professional reputation and goodwill.' It alleged charges related to injurious falsehood, defamation, malicious prosecution, abuse of process and conspiracy. But Veritas stopped in its tracks once the Delhi High Court on 25 September restrained it from proceeding with the Canadian suit till the case was next heard in India in February 2015. Since one court cannot direct another court to stall proceedings, the litigants (Veritas and Mongia) were ordered to stay put by way of an anti-suit injunction. In May 2015, Indiabulls filed a suit against Veritas and Monga seeking ₹200 crore in damages for submissions made in Ontario.

In September 2015, Veritas and Monga move the Ontario Superior Court of Justice seeking relief against the Delhi High Court proceedings. The plea did not work—on 2 October 2015, the Ontario court dismissed the anti-suit injunction proceeding and also criticised the Canadian research firm's decision not to respond to proceedings in Indian courts. This made Veritas appear through its lawyer three days later in the suit for ₹200 crore of damages.

Meanwhile, Monga who had a stake in Veritas moved out of the company and floated his own entity called Antya Investment Research. It was Mangal who kept waging a lonely battle from the back of the financial beyonds—in Indore, Madhya Pradesh. He was finally granted bail by the Gurgaon sessions court on 11 December 2014.

The Veritas-Indiabulls case raised many appropriate questions. Could a market researcher and analyst be put behind bars solely on the basis of a report he had written? Many thought the actions were unconscionable; Mangal had only been a researcher, and had merely fished out data and reports for the Veritas study.

Devangshu Datta, columnist with a focus on financial markets, felt that going after the messenger did send a signal to the market. But, as he pointed out to the writers of this book, 'The 'wrong/right' signal is a difficult one to judge. From the group perspective, it might be signalling 'Look we have enough clout to shut people up; this also means we have enough clout to get our business done'. Given that India is a crony-capitalistic environment, this might well be seen as a right signal.'

He then went on to explain, 'Financial analysis is often amoral since it tries to answer a basic question: Will my capital grow/shrink if it is invested in X (whoever/whatever X may be)? Any analysis has to be taken in that context. Say, X is a crook, but he's a crook who 'gets things done'—that is probably seen as a good thing in the context of the Indian investment environment where the entire regulatory environment is very complex and administered by crooks. You do need to know if X is a man/woman of his word, and also how minority shareholders are treated. But any Indian investor accepts that corners will be cut.'

Nevertheless, Indiabulls remained obstinate: it was not willing to even read about the original Veritas report anywhere in the media; it wanted gag orders.

The Delhi High Court on 1 May 2015 restrained the *Wall Street Journal* and one of its senior reporters—2003 Pulitzer Prize winner Geeta Anand—from publishing any article on the Indiabulls group on matters relating to the research report published by Veritas and the subsequent legal tussle. This order was in response to an application moved by Indiabulls Real Estate, alleging Anand had sent it a 'threatening email' and was about to publish a 'defamatory' article on the group. In the order, Justice Jayanth Nath said, 'In my view, the plaintiff has made out a *prima facie* case in its favour. Balance of convenience is also in favour of the plaintiff and against the defendants. The defendants are restrained by an *ex parte ad interim* injunction from publishing, disseminating or broadcasting reports pertaining to and arising out of the *Bilking India* report dated 1 August 2012, or any other connected reports defaming the plaintiff till further orders.'

A two-judge bench of the high court on 9 June 2015 upheld an appeal by Anand against the earlier order. However, the relief was for only the reporter. WSJ publisher Dow Jones, which had not appealed, remained bound by the earlier restraint order. On 7 September, two days before the Bombay High Court threw out the NSE complaint against Sucheta Dalal and *MoneyLife*, the Delhi High Court disposed of the Indiabulls petition.

The court remarked, 'We have heard the counsel for the parties. The counsel agreed the order, dated 16 April and passed by the single judge, be modified to the extent the appellant would be free to publish the article subject to their complying with the norms of journalistic conduct.' It directed Indiabulls to respond to questions sent by Anand. 'A questionnaire has been sent by Geeta Anand to respondent no.1 in these appeals through emails dated 14 April and 27 July. It has been agreed that the respondent no.1 in these appeals shall give response to Geeta Anand on or before 10 am (IST) on 14 September. In view of the above order, the appeals stand disposed of.' The reporter and the newspaper were thus free to write and report.

The *Wall Street Journal* carried the detailed article on 16 September 2015, chronicling the ordeals of Mangal who told Anand, 'I feared for my life. I did not know what they would do to me.' Mangal spoke about how he was taken on a long road trip by the police, allegedly accompanied by an Indiabulls lawyer by the name of Ajay Grewal. Mangal claimed he was asked to sign an affidavit blaming Veritas, in return for which was he was offered a job and dropping of charges against him, the report said.

The chief executive of Indiabulls, Gagan Banga, did not respond personally to the reporter's emails. Instead, a company executive replied with a detailed note of the ongoing legal proceedings. The note alleged that Mangal's assertion against Grewal was only an afterthought. It hinted at cornering the former Veritas researcher once again, 'Nitin Mangal has clearly flouted the order of the Delhi High Court (of 16 April) by providing commentary, making statements and posing for pictures for the WSJ article dated September 15. It is a clear case of contempt of the orders of the Delhi High Court and the company will press for fresh charges of contempt of court in this regard.'

The Veritas-Indiabulls case had its share of chilling effects too. Barring a few, most newspapers and other news establishments steered clear of Mangal. Except for the routine news items about developments in the legal tussle (ongoing at the time of this book going to the press), nothing much was heard of.

Not just reporting or researching, even analysing and commenting on issues related to financial markets can land one in trouble. Or at least harassed, ceaselessly at that.

An example of this, executed in copybook style, was the hounding of economist Ajay Shah by the Multi-Commodities Exchange (MCX) and its chief Jignesh Shah. All that Ajay Shah, a professor with the National Institute of Public Finance and Policy (NIPFP) in New Delhi, had done was air his views about the need for stricter market regulations. His contention was this: MCX may have been successful because it operated in an area where regulation was weak. Commodities were at that time regulated by the Forward Markets Commission (FMC), which unlike SEBI did not have the necessary authority to discipline and penalise players with clout. The FMC was to be later merged with SEBI in November 2014.

In an article in the *Financial Express on 4 February 2009*, Shah wrote:

> In the areas of the economy where regulation is necessary, a careful configuration of legal foundations, regulator, corporate governance of regulated entities and public discourse is required. When these ingredients are lacking, 'regulatory capture' comes about, where the actions of regulators favour one player over another. The recent episode of FMC preventing NCDEX [National Commodity and Derivatives Exchange] from cutting prices is an example: the only beneficiary of FMC's action is the incumbent, MCX, which aspires to do an IPO. Making progress requires laying sound legal foundations, setting up high quality regulators, requiring good corporate governance practices, and having open discussion of these difficult issues.

Shah raised concerns. He argued that the FMC was not independent from the political system, and that 'MCX operates in an area—commodity futures—where the legal foundations and the regulator are weak.'

> MCX competes with an exchange named NCDEX. The smaller exchange, NCDEX, cut prices in trying to gain market share. Ordinarily, in a duopoly, when one player cuts prices, the other is likely to follow resulting in benefits for customers. In this case, the special twist lies in the fact that MCX has long planned to do an IPO. The valuation that MCX can obtain in the IPO will reflect the net present value of the profit that it can make in coming years. MCX is probably keen to stave off a price reduction.

> Normally, a regulator would applaud a price cut, since elevated prices are precisely what regulation seeks to prevent. In this case,

FMC went beyond its legal brief and ordered NCDEX to raise prices. NCDEX has taken FMC to court.

As an economist, Shah was disturbed about systemic flaws:

When regulation is weak, this encourages the players who have strengths in fixing the regulatory system to their own advantage. The firms that have risen to prominence in such areas in India tend to be those who were unable to compete in global markets under fair competition. Even a few years of faulty regulation can do long-term damage to an industry, by killing off firms with high ethical standards and endowed with skills in running a business as opposed to skills in fixing the system.

Ajay Shah had earlier articulated the need for a three-way separation between owners, managers and trading members in the *Business Standard* on 17 May 2006. He had mentioned MCX's proposed initial public offering (IPO) in the context:

The question of listed exchanges is now a live one in India. The MCX seeks to do an IPO. A recent SEBI report says that regional stock exchanges should do IPOs and list on themselves. The BSE could get listed, possibly on the BSE. But exchanges are not ordinary firms, where we applaud when the firm graduates from startup to IPO. Listed exchanges pose daunting policy questions. SEBI and the MoF [ministry of finance] need to do deep thinking about whether India's interests are best served by a three-way separation between owners, managers and brokers.

In the bad old days, an exchange was a club of brokers. It was run by brokers, in the best interests of brokers. This led to malpractice. Today, we know that what works best is a three-way separation between owners, managers and trading members. The pioneers in this new 'demutualised' framework were the Stockholm Exchange (1993) and India's NSE [National Stock Exchange] (1994). Over the years, most major global exchanges have moved towards this structure to some extent or the other.

Why does this work better? The managers have their reputations to protect, they only earn a salary, and have no financial interest in profits of either exchange or members. This helps them be impartial.

MCX did not take kindly to the columnist's comments, and filed a defamation case in Mumbai on 24 April 2009, citing the earlier *Business Standard* article as a precedent. Shah aired similar views during a programme on the CNBC Aawaz television channel, and attracted a criminal case that was filed on 16 July 2011 of all places in Kolhapur, 376km from Mumbai.

In the meantime, Shah wrote a blog post on SEBI's consent order on certain irregularities in the trading of shares of Reliance Communications. In doing so, he made a passing reference to MCX-SX (MCX Stock Exchange Limited, later renamed Metropolitan Stock Exchange of India Limited, or MSEI):

> This order is one more pillar in the body of case law of CB Bhave's SEBI.[25] I think of Bhave's achievement at SEBI as being a series of remarkable orders. SEBI is a quasi-judicial organisation and the technical quality of this organisation is all about the quality of orders that they are able to come up with. Alongside other famous orders—Sahara, MCX-SX, HDFC AMC front running, ULIPs, Bank of Rajasthan, Pyramid Saimira—this is a major achievement of SEBI in nailing wrong-doing and (more importantly) scaring off other would-be wrongdoers. For each firm that is visible as

---

25 Chandrasekhar Bhaskar Bhave was chairman of the Securities and Exchange Board of India (SEBI) for three years starting February 2008. Earlier, he had been SEBI's senior executive director from 1992 to 1996. After this stint, Bhave became chairman and managing director of the just-created National Securities Depository Limited (NSDL).

having been caught trying to violate rules, there are ten other entrepreneurs who have been dissuaded from similar business strategies by watching these events unfold.

In the 6 September 2010 order on MCX-SX, adjudicating officer KM Abraham wrote: 'I have little hesitation in holding that MCX-SX has been dishonest in its disclosures to SEBI on material information and has failed to fulfil its disclosure and fiduciary responsibilities cast on it under Regulation 11 of the MIMPS Regulations (MIMPS is Manner of Increasing and Maintaining Public Shareholding in Recognised Exchanges Regulations 2006).' Abraham was the same officer who had complained to Prime Minister Manmohan Singh of pressures from the finance ministry (headed by Pranab Mukherjee) in high-profile cases, including those concerning the Sahara India Pariwar and MCX. Incidentally, the court ruling later went in favour of MCX.

The blog post of 18 February 2011 met with the same reaction, with MCX filing a case on 24 June 2011 in Surat.

Three separate cases in different cities was harassment enough, and was possibly meant to serve that precise purpose. *Firstpost* editor R Jagannathan commented: 'Suing a man three times over in three different places can reasonably be considered a way of harassing him. *Firstpost*, which believes in a writer's freedom to argue his points, however harshly, believes that MCX is effectively trying to muzzle Shah, an outspoken advocate for free markets, which is what MCX too apparently believes in, since it took the NSE to the Competition Commission of India (CCI) for predatory pricing in currency futures.'

MCX reacted to the *Firstpost* article as well, contending that the facts pertaining to Jignesh Shah and MCX had been misrepresented:

With regard to Ajay Shah's article 'The X factor in regulation' please note that the statements made are slanderous and defamatory in nature. The imputation clearly suggests that MCX is taking illegitimate advantage of allegedly weak legal and regulatory foundations in conducting its business activities. The article also alleges that MCX has skills 'in fixing the system' as opposed to skills 'in running a business.' The article insinuates MCX as being a beneficiary of FMC's action of preventing NCDEX from cutting price.

Jagannathan's response to MCX was bereft of rhetoric and all for the free airing of views: '*Firstpost* has no axe to grind for or against MCX. Our only interest was in pointing out what we believe is excessive legal response to a sharp critique through three different courts. In the interest of wider debate on the issues involved, public corporations should be more tolerant of dissent and criticism, even if they think it is motivated. A public rebuttal of Ajay Shah's views would have been more than adequate in this case.'

The same sentiments were penned by other writers and commentators. Former chief economic consultant to the finance ministry Ashok Desai asserted in a op-ed in the *Telegraph* that a writer should have the freedom to express an opinion about a public matter. 'Public debate is essential for judging a public body and MCX is a public body.' That MCX was trying to stifle criticism was not taken kindly by most.

The quirk of fate in this case lay elsewhere—the law caught up with Jignesh Shah. Shah and his long-time colleague Shreekant Javalgekar were on 7 May 2014 arrested by the economic offences wing of the Mumbai police in connection with the ₹5,600 crore payment fraud at the National Spot Exchange Ltd (NSEL). Shah, founder and promoter of Financial Technologies India Ltd (FTIL),

and Javalgekar, former managing director and chief executive of
MCX were charged with being involved in criminal conspiracy.

The NSEL scam, as it was popularly referred to, came to light
on 31 July 2013 when it was found that most of the underlying
commodities (which were supposed to be traded) did not exist
and the buying and selling of commodities like steel, paddy,
sugar, ferrochrome, etc, were being conducted only on paper. The
NSEL was promoted as a spot commodity exchange by FTIL and
a token 100 shares were given to NAFED [National Agricultural
Cooperative Marketing Federation of India Ltd] so that the latter's
brand name could be used and the exchange could be described
as a 'farmer's market.' The NSEL had managed to get a specific
exemption under the Forward Contracts Regulation Act (FCRA),
1952 from the ministry of consumer affairs in 2007, then headed
by Sharad Pawar. This exemption was only for all one-day forward
contracts up to 11 days. Between 2007 and 2009, the NSEL with full
knowledge of Jignesh Shah and other board members introduced
fraudulent 'paired contracts' whereby investors could buy short
duration contracts and sell long duration contracts at the same
time. Both the FMC and the ministry concerned knew that these
contracts were illegal, but remained tight-lipped. The immediate
cause of arrest of Jignesh Shah was his knowledge of dealings of
the Indian Bullion Markets Association (IBMA), a subsidiary of
NSEL which was predominantly used in money laundering and
bogus trades.

As skeletons kept tumbling out, the context of MCX's relentless
pursuit of Ajay Shah became clear. The *Caravan* in its November
2014 cover story 'A Shah Overthrown' made it more intelligible:

> Regulatory capture is a case of gamekeeper turning poacher—of
> a public body controlled by the industry it is supposed to oversee.
> In 2004, the two main exchanges regulated by the FMC were

the rival bourses of the NSE and Financial Technologies. For anyone familiar with Ajay Shah's opinion pieces, it would have been clear that he meant that interests aligned with the MCX were dominating the FMC. If he didn't come straight out and say this, he had good reason. Financial Technologies had had him in its crosshairs since at least 2009, when he wrote an article in the *Financial Express* essentially alleging that the commission had been captured by Financial Technologies and the MCX.

With the soft-pedalling on these allegations by Pranab Mukherjee as also the uncloaked patronage showered by Pawar disappearing with the ousting of the Congress-led United Progressive Alliance (UPA) government, the noose tightened around Jignesh Shah. On 28 February 2015, the ministry of corporate affairs, convinced about FTIL's fraudulent activities, moved a Company Law Board (CLB) application to take over the board of FTIL and replace it with government-nominated directors. With Jignesh Shah out of the way, MCX dropped its cases against Ajay Shah.

The harassment of Ajay Shah ended, but more by default. The questions that he had raised—especially that of better and transparent regulations—did not go away. If his allegations were misplaced, those could have been simply rebutted. Putting a man in jail, as would have been the intention of MCX through its criminal defamation cases, for an analysis or an opinion, whosoever incorrect or motivated, cannot possibly be acceptable in a civilised society. This rings all the more true for public bodies and those dealing with public monies.

The financial markets will surely see more fiercely-contested tussles in the days to come. This will possibly be boosted by public interest in the way businesses and well-entrenched individuals make the best of loopholes in the law. The furore over the Offshore Leaks of May 2014 and the Panama Papers investigations of April

2016 that were carried out by the International Consortium of Investigative Journalists (ICIJ), with the *Indian Express* being its Indian partner, could well signal the beginning of a trend—that of financial journalism turning more investigative and data-driven in nature.

Those journalists following the money trail always come up with good stories. Of course, not everyone likes such stories—especially those inconvenienced by scrupulous data mining.

6

Poison All Around

In 1962, American marine biologist and conservationist Rachel Carson published *Silent Spring*, a seminal work that lugged environmental concerns into the mainstream. Her book documented the detrimental effects in the indiscriminate use of pesticides on the environment, especially on birds. *Silent Spring* argued that the chemicals industry in the United States was spreading disinformation, and that public officials were unquestioningly swallowing up industry claims. The impact of the book is today reckoned to be legion—the US not only did a turnaround on its pesticides policy including banning dichloro-diphenyl-trichloroethane (DDT) and other pesticides, the mass awareness generated by *Silent Spring* in time led to the establishment of the Environmental Protection Agency (EPA) in 1970.

Pesticides and other toxic chemicals are still used around the world, though usage since then has fallen drastically in many countries, specially those in the West. India, for its part however, still does not have a policy on pesticides. The linkages between pesticides (the only toxic substances released intentionally into the environment to kill living things) on the one hand, and environment and human health on the other, are largely ignored by policymakers. If there is one area in environmental reportage that meets with belligerent and virulent opposition in India, it is the subject of pesticides. It is no surprise that the history of critical reportage and journalistic writing on the subject is riddled with cases of litigation.

The most significant of these is the one that followed a series of investigative reports published by the *Rajasthan Patrika* in early 2004. The first on 12 February 2004 highlighted the harmful effects of pesticides and insecticides on human health, and contended that vegetables available in different parts of Rajasthan state were highly contaminated with a number of prohibited chemicals. The second report, a day later, delved into the question as to why the farmers were using intemperate levels of insecticides and pesticides in their agricultural practices. The ruse that came through was this: the practice was a result of the personal greed of the people involved. This report also pointed out the detrimental effects on soil and water as a fallout of the overuse or misuse of these chemicals. The third article, on 15 February, focused on fruits and made similar assertions, while the fourth on 16 February fixed the responsibility for the crises on various governmental departments including agriculture, pollution control, health and food. The report on the next day spoke of the state government's plans to deal with the situation (arising out of the use of pesticides), while the concluding report on 22 February was about the Union government's plans to inquire into the issue. This news item also reported about the resolve of hundreds of peasants not to use pesticides or insecticides in the future. Overall, journalistically speaking, it was an exhaustive coverage of a contentious issue. Moreover, it was about an issue that would have touched the lives of every citizen.

The entity that did not agree with the reportage was the Crop

Care Federation of India (CCFI), a company incorporated by guarantee and claiming to be a non-profit organisation. The CCFI took the newspaper, its publisher, editor, advisor and reporters to court. It said the articles had the 'tendency to lower its reputation' and those of its 84 members, and claimed damages of ₹50 lakh. The case was fought not in Rajasthan, but in the Delhi High Court. The battle dragged on for years, and when the single-judge bench of Justice S Ravindra Bhat gave its ruling, it went on to become a landmark judgment.

It was possibly the first time that the term SLAPP (strategic lawsuit against public participation) was used in a major court ruling in India, and the judgment even went to the extent of describing the action of CCFI as a SLAPP suit. Judge Bhat on 27 November 2009 remarked, 'A number of jurisdictions have made such suits illegal. The plaintiff's attempt, in the opinion of the court, by filing the suit here in Delhi, in relation to publications in Rajasthan, on what were matters of public concern, but called for debate, was to muffle the airing of such views. The suit was not brought by a company really aggrieved, as a manufacturer, who alone could have claimed a cause of action, but virtually a trade body, though created as a company limited by guarantee. The attempt was plainly to stifle debate about the use of pesticides and insecticides. Whether such use, or overuse of pesticides over a period of time, affects life, plant or human, could be a matter of discourse, but certainly not one which could be stifled through intimidatory SLAPP litigation.'

In the penultimate paragraph of his 29-para ruling, Justice Bhat spoke of the perils of SLAPPs, 'Free speech and expression is the life blood of democracy. Any action—even civil injunctions, damages, or threat to damages, are bound to chill the exercise of that invaluable right of the people, and the press. By giving such orders, or allowing claims for damages, for perceived injury to reputation, the harm done to freedom of press, which facilitates free flow of ideas is incalculable.'

What led the judge to make such critical remarks were essentially the very reasons under which the plaint was rejected. He said in the ruling, 'Order 7 Rule 11 CPC (Code of Civil Procedure) requires the cause of action to be disclosed. This means that in the plaint, there must be averments, which disclose the cause of action. Disclosure of the cause of action would necessarily mean that the ingredients/essentials are satisfied through the averments. Thus for an action of defamation to be maintainable, the plaint must contain averments, which satisfy the essentials for an action of defamation and thereby completely disclose the cause of action.' Under Indian law, a civil suit is filed by presenting a plaint. If the plaint is defective on any of the six grounds mentioned in Order 7 Rule 11 CPC, the plaint can be rejected by the court.

The judge referred to a 1977 Supreme Court judgment wherein it had held that 'if on a meaningful—not formal—reading of the plaint it is manifestly found to be vexatious and meritless, in the sense of not disclosing a right to sue, the judge should exercise his power under Order 7 Rule 11 CPC taking care to see that the ground mentioned therein is fulfilled.' The keywords here were 'vexatious' and 'meritless.' The same spirit of the law had been referred to by the apex court subsequently in a 1988 judgment wherein it said in no uncertain terms, 'Question is whether a real cause of action has been set out in the plaint or something purely illusory has been stated with the view to get out of Order 7 Rule 11 CPC. Clever drafting of creating illusions are not permitted in law and a clear right to sue should be shown in the plaint.'

The usage of 'vexatious' in Justice Bhat's ruling was significant. In legal parlance, a vexatious litigant is the proponent of an action that is brought about without sufficient grounds for winning, and purely to cause annoyance to the defendant. This is where the SLAPP mention in the judgment assumed significance.

There were other significant aspects about the Delhi High Court judgment. One question that emerged was whether CCFI could indeed speak on behalf of all its members and the industry too. The judge pointed out, 'The plaintiff is a distinct company, having its juristic entity, separate from its members; they in turn are companies, firms, etc. The said entities—who manufacture insecticides and pesticides have not chosen to step forward to air their grievances. It is not as if they labour under a disability from suing for the alleged defamation. In these circumstances, the plaintiff cannot assume the role of a *parens patriae* (the principle that political authority carries with it the responsibility for such protection) and sue, virtually on their behalf.' CCFI could institute a suit on behalf of its members only after disclosing all the potential plaintiffs, and following the procedure spelt out in Order 1 Rule 8 CPC.

The action of CCFI, claiming to speak on behalf of the entire industry, was questioned by the court on other grounds too. Justice Bhat said, 'It is a settled position that when it is written that 'all lawyers are liars' or 'all religious heads are simulators,' no particular person occupying that position can sue the writer unless he can establish that the words were pointed at him. On the other hand, if a defamatory statement is made referring to a certain group of people, e.g. tenants of a particular building, then such tenants against whom the statement is made will generally be able to sue. The thin line of difference between the two types of cases is that in the latter type the plaintiff can be identified as the target of the alleged defamation, while in the former he cannot be so identified. The present case falls into the first category and thus no action against the defendants lie in favour of the plaintiff.'

Even while the CCFI vs *Rajasthan Patrika* case was on, the industry organisation was locked in another battle, the roots of which predated the former by a good two years.

In October 2001, the Delhi-based Toxics Link and Hyderabad-based Centre for Resource Education decided to ascertain the authenticity of a report emanating from Warangal district of Andhra Pradesh. The report was about the Andhra Pradesh Raithu Sangham, a farmer's organisation with a state-wide network, talking about deaths of farmers while applying pesticides on cotton crops. The state secretary of the organisation, Sarampalli Malla Reddy, claimed to have seen hospital records showing deaths caused by the spraying of pesticides. Members of the two organisations, along with one of Sarvodaya Youth Organisation, visited the area, and *prima facie* confirmed deaths caused by the use of pesticides. From the discussions from this preliminary trip, it was evident that a more in-depth analysis was required.

In the second week of January 2002, representatives of the three organisations along with one from the Bengaluru-based Community Health Cell, made a hectic three-day fact-finding visit to six mandals in the district.[26] The indicative 32-page report of the team, titled *The Killing Fields of Warangal* and published later that month, clearly laid out, 'Qualitative methods like focused group discussions, questionnaires were used while conducting field investigations to ensure uniform information collection and credibility of the investigation. The fact-finding team's visit was

---

26 A mandal is an administrative division in some Indian states. It is an area constituting a city/town that serves as the administrative centre, with possible additional towns, and usually a number of villages. Also known as 'tehsil' or 'taluk(a)' in certain states.

not aimed at doing [a] health study or [an] in-depth scientific investigation, but to do an indicative study which would lead to a larger health study.'

The team found that majority of the individuals affected by pesticide exposure were farm labourers working for their employers, and the others were marginal farmers, with 1–5 acres of land holdings on an average. The victims were from an economically insecure background, with almost no coverage for medical expenditure. The interactions with the farmers and their family members were meticulously documented, and the report dwelt at length on the adverse health effects that were narrated to the researchers. The activists were convinced that an in-depth health study needed to be conducted, not only in Warangal but also in neighbouring Guntur district, where pesticide consumption was the highest in the country. They categorically asserted in the report, 'This assessment should include health impacts on women and children in particular and should also encompass other specific social sections like farm labourers and marginal farmers.'

The fact-finding team put the situation down in numbers: 'On the basis of preliminary investigation by the team, taking into account 2–3 deaths and more than 5–10 cases of exposure in villages visited and increase in the acreage under cotton this year to all mandals in the district, it is estimated that there could be more than 500 deaths in Warangal district, and more than 1,000 exposed in the period between August to December 2001. This needs to be further investigated to get the correct estimates.' The team also called for a detailed investigation into similar experiences elsewhere in the country, and the formulation of a comprehensive national pesticide policy that would focus on rational use of pesticides, control and strict monitoring of accessibility to such dangerous chemicals, and a gradual phase-out of chemical pesticides.

Of all people, it was the CCFI which again took umbrage to the findings and recommendations. The organisation initiated criminal proceedings against the members of the fact-finding team and others associated with the publishing of the report, stating that it was a malicious and defamatory attempt by the members of the team to defame the pesticide manufacturers and traders among the general public, thereby affecting their credibility and their business. The grouse had been virtually the same as in the case with the *Rajasthan Patrika*. In this instance, the proceedings were initiated in a Warangal magistrate's court, which even issued non-bailable arrest warrants against some of the accused in 2007 after the Andhra Pradesh High Court dismissed an appeal to quash the proceedings. The tussle moved on to the Supreme Court.

Acting on a special leave petition (SLP), the apex court quashed the defamation proceedings. The brief judgment of the two-judge bench of Justices Dalveer Bhandari and Deepak Verma on 20 July 2010 was telling in import, and far-reaching in consequence: 'We have carefully perused the report. The relevant page of the report, which is at page 40 of the paper book, clearly indicates that the fact-finding committee was not aimed at doing [a] health study or in-depth scientific investigation, but to do an indicative study which would lead to a larger health study. The general tenor of the report indicates that the report meant to focus [on] the harmful effects of exposure to pesticides. It is quite evident from the report that it was not meant to harm, hurt or defame any individual or the manufacturing company.'

In a matter of eight months, the CCFI had lost two major defamation cases—both seen by detractors as SLAPPs. The curious thing here was that the federation's chairman, Rajju Shroff, was himself involved in another long-drawn legal tussle through his own company, United Phosphorus Limited (UPL), which was later rechristened UPL Limited.

This particular instance was the result of a feature written by photo-journalist Shailendra Yashwant, who visited Vapi, an industrial estate on the Gujarat-Maharashtra border, to examine the site of a proposed toxic chemical plant being imported into India from Norway. He filed the report in May 1995 after discussions with locals, experts and officials of UPL for Sanctuary Features, a Mumbai-based environmental features agency. The article was carried in *News Time* magazine (now defunct) and *Mid-Day* newspaper. The latter did its own editorialising and sensationalising by mangling the story and retaining only the UPL angle. *Mid-Day* subsequently ran an apology followed by a fulsome feature on how UPL had brought prosperity to Vapi.

Headlined 'Colours of Death', the article shot off in no uncertain words, 'United Phosphorus, a Bombay based agro-chemical company has imported a moth balled and very hazardous chlor-alkali plant into India. The plant obtained from Norway-based Norske Skog will produce organochlorines and chlorinated organophosphorous pesticides. According to Kenny Bruno and Geir Wang Anderson of Greenpeace the plant was up for sale because it was shut down in 1992 under strong pressure from environmentalists in Norway. Organochlorines as a group tend to be toxic, persistent and bio-accumulative—the body cannot get rid of them. Agent Orange, DDT and ozone depleting chlorflurocarbons are some infamous compounds of organochlorine processes. The adverse health effects of organochlorines include cancer, birth defects, reproductive and development impairments and hormonal disruption.'

The report also raked up allegations concerning UPL's past: 'The Indian company which has been allowed by the government to bring in the toxic unit has a dubious past. The 260-crore company, with chemical factories at Vapi and Ankleshwar in Gujarat was accused of having exported chemicals capable of producing nerve gas to Iraq. Recently the firm hit the headlines again when a shipment of trimethyl phosphite to Syria was intercepted and returned by German coast guards. TMP, a dual-purpose chemical, is used to manufacture pesticides and is also an intermediate to produce nerve gas.'

UPL hauled Yashwant to the Mumbai's additional chief metropolitan magistrate's court. The case is still being played out. Yashwant did not speak to the authors of this book since the matter was still *sub judice* when this book went to the press. A number of facts could, nevertheless, be dug out from other sources.

It definitely had been the open toxic effluent drain and the colourful sludge mountains on the banks of Damanganga river that piqued the journalist's interest, since he would regularly travel to Baroda in the early 1990s to cover the Narmada Bachao Andolan's activities for the *Hindu* and *Frontline*, and every time the train went over the river, he would see a lethal cocktail of effluents flowing under the bridge.

Defamation notices in the 1990s were not that commonplace; Yashwant was left disturbed on being served one. This had been only his third environmental feature as a freelancer and pitching stories to editors would no more be that easy. Yet, it was not that Yashwant was a stranger to notices. He had got one for a *Frontline* story about the Adani Group clearing vast swathes of mangroves and displacing ancient settlements to set up a port in Mundra, Gujarat in 1994. The Adani Group at that time was not that big, and the notice fizzled out. Yashwant was to later work for *Outlook* and Greenpeace India, but the UPL case is still going on. For almost 20 years now.

Vapi too was to meet its own fate. In 2011, the Union ministry of environment and forests (MoEF) identified six critically polluted industrial clusters in Gujarat, including Bhavnagar and Junagadh in Saurashtra, Vapi and Ankleshwar in South Gujarat and Ahmedabad and Vatva in Central Gujarat. A moratorium was imposed by the ministry on the clusters for critically polluting nature. The state government has since been lobbying hard with the Centre for a lifting of the moratorium.

Greenpeace, which ran campaigns against toxics in Vapi, meanwhile had run-ins with both CCFI and UPL. On 30 September 2006, a Valsad court in Gujarat asked Greenpeace to pay ₹48 lakh as damages to the Vapi-based Chemi Organics. Principal senior civil judge GC Gamit noted in his judgment: 'It is humbly submitted that the defendants (Greenpeace activists) miserably failed to prove that the statements made in the defamatory article are true and they have also failed to prove that they have made fair comments after making proper and diligent enquiry...' London-based Greenpeace International activists David Santillo and Bob Edwards had in November 1996 published a report titled *The Stranger*, alleging that the chemicals industry in Vapi and Ankleshwar was polluting the environment. They had claimed to have collected samples of sludge waste from outside the factory site of Chemi Organics, one of the largest producers of chloro-benzene in India. The allegations incidentally were also contested by UPL.

Later, on 11 August 2014, Greenpeace India launched a report *Trouble Brewing: Pesticide Residues in Tea Samples from India* alleging the presence of pesticides, considered highly and moderately hazardous by the World Health Organization (WHO), in leading national and international tea brands. The report also revealed the presence of other pesticides which had not been approved for use on tea crops in India.

Greenpeace said at the launch, 'The study results indicate

that the tea sector is caught in a pesticide treadmill and the only way out is ecological farming. Greenpeace India is calling on tea companies to support this change. All the companies named in our report have been contacted and we have been interacting with them over the last several months. The copies of the test results were also shared. We also requested the companies to adopt a time-bound roadmap starting with pilots to phase out pesticides in their supply chains and replace them with ecological agriculture methods, such as non-pesticidal management. We also urged them to disclose the names and locations of the plantations from where they source their tea and set targets for procuring ecological tea. Further we urged them to liaise with relevant government bodies to develop support systems for small tea growers to adopt pesticide free farming.'

The backlash came eight days later—in the form of a legal notice, not from the tea industry but—from CCFI. It contended that the report was 'fabricated' and 'pseudo-scientific'. Shroff even told the media, 'We have sent a legal notice to Greenpeace for creating panic in the Indian consumer's mind by publishing a false report of pesticides in tea brands and discredit Indian agro products.' The notice asked Greenpeace to furnish all raw data collected and analysed for the study and tender an unconditional apology within seven days, failing which a defamation case for ₹50 crore would be filed.

The backing for CCFI came surprisingly from the home ministry. A news report in the first half of April 2015 said the ministry had alleged that Greenpeace was trying to hurt the Indian tea industry, which employed 35 lakh workers and earned $644 million from exports the previous financial year, by projecting abroad that homegrown leaves of the beverage contained hazardous pesticides. A ministry report contended, 'It (Greenpeace) claims to have identified hazardous pesticides in leading Indian tea brands, all of which are exported in large quantities to the US, UK and Europe. The Tea Board of India has disagreed with the above findings and sees it as an attempt to impact Indian tea exports. The anti-tea Greenpeace campaign is similar to the one against Chinese tea companies.' The allegations were in the same vein as CCFI had been making against all environmental activists working in the areas of pesticides and toxics.

Soon, CCFI took the argument forward, by filing a criminal defamation case against Greenpeace India before a metropolitan magistrate's court in suburban Bandra on 3 May. The complaint contended, 'Greenpeace India and its members have made several defamatory statements against the tea industry as well as pesticides industry in the defamatory report. These remarks are highly defamatory to the manufacturers and marketers of pesticides in India who have suffered loss of reputation amongst their buyers, distributors and the public at large.' It argued that Greenpeace had made defamatory imputations and innuendos against CCFI and its members. 'The said imputations and innuendos have caused great injury to the impeccable reputation of CCFI. In spite of calling upon Greenpeace for retraction of the defamatory report, they have failed to do so,' the federation said. The Tea Board too denied Greenpeace's allegations, as did other tea biggies, but none of them went to the extent of filing defamation charges.

The other organisation that CCFI has consistently been at daggers drawn with is the New Delhi-based environmental organisation, Centre for Science and Environment (CSE).[27] In May 2006, the organisation's director-general Sunita Narain

---

27 **Disclosure:** One of the authors of this book, Subir Ghosh, worked in the publications department of the Centre for Science and Environment (CSE) from July 1998 till March 1999.

wrote an editorial about SLAPP suits in *Down To Earth* magazine, published by the Society for Environmental Communications, an associate of CSE. Narain wrote of a YS Mohana Kumar, a doctor practising in Padre village of Kasaragod district in Kerala. What Mohana Kumar noticed was that the people in his village were more diseased and deformed than others. That got him asking questions, uncomfortable ones for sure.

Researchers in due course confirmed the presence of residues of the pesticide called endosulfan in the blood, soil and water samples from the village. In 2003, Mohana Kumar received a notice threatening legal action if he did not apologise and withdraw his statements immediately. All that Mohana Kumar had done was write a letter (to the editor) about the findings in *Down To Earth*. He wrote against the OP Dubey Committee which had absolved the pesticide of deleterious effects. The magazine followed up the story and found how data had been fudged and scientists coerced, and how industry had influenced the working of the committee. The proceedings were challenged and investigations reopened by the Union government.

Narain had more in her editorial:

Umendra Dutt runs an NGO in Punjab called Kheti Virasat Mission, which works on various farmer-related issues, including pesticide use. He has been sued for ₹5 crore by United Phosphorus Limited, a leading pesticide manufacturer. His crime: discussing in public, health studies on pesticide exposure and how it could act as a trigger to diseases, and even lead to congenital malformations and genetic disorders. All clearly well-established in scientific studies across the world.

But it does not stop there. The company has also filed a case against the media giant, Bennett and Coleman, the publishers of the *Times of India*. Their crime is similar: publishing a report quoting Dutt

in their daily newspaper, *Mumbai Mirror*. The defamation case
has been filed by the company alleging that the statements in the
article will 'disparage our client's reputation' in the trade across
the world. This is particularly intriguing, because the article does
not mention the company at all, only pesticides and their health
impacts.

But how did Narain know all this?

> Because two weeks ago, my colleague Chandra Bhushan, received
> a letter from an NGO called the Centre for Environment and
> Agrochemicals, which enclosed a copy of this legal notice. The
> letter told him that if he was to attend a forthcoming meeting
> being organised by Kheti Virasat Mission he 'will be made a party
> (to the case against Kheti Virasat) and unnecessarily dragged into
> litigation.' In simple language a simple threat: we will sue you if
> you dare to attend.

> It does not stop there. We called to check more about the NGO
> and received another letter. The letterhead was the same, but the
> signatory had changed. Now Rajju Shroff, the owner of United
> Phosphorus Limited wrote, saying, 'The industry has decided to
> take legal actions and expose all your activities.' I am sure we will
> hear from them again.

And that, she did. At one point, a group of men protested outside
the CSE office in the Tughlakabad Extension area of New Delhi,
and distributed a booklet titled *Chemistry of a Scientific Fraud*.
They carried placards, and shouted slogans against Narain. She
wrote another editorial, this one on how CCFI first targeted CSE's
research and then her:

> In all this time, even as we refused to give in to the threats, we also
> respected their right to protest. This time, too, we decided to leave
> the picket alone. Then, a few days into the 'protest,' a journalist

with a city daily visited and recognised one of the protesters outside our gate. This was not an employee of the aggrieved pesticide company or a protesting NGO, he said. This man was a representative of a public relations company who had met him, on behalf of biscuit manufacturers, to make the case that government should allow processed food, instead of cooked hot meals, in the multi-crore school meal programme.

We were puzzled. Surely, Indian industry was too proud or forthright to hire protesters? Why would reputed public relations companies engage in dirty tricks and intimidation? We knew this kind of thing happened in the US, where corporations hired lobbyists and white collared goons. But was this now happening in India? We decided to investigate.

When we checked with all known names in the public relations business, nobody had heard of this company—Media Expressions Consortium. Finally, when my colleagues tracked it down to a small office based in a Mumbai suburb, a sinister canister of worms leaked out. The company, we learnt, represented the biggest of the polluters—the plastic industry and pesticide industry—as well as others, like the biscuit manufacturers, to defend their interests. The company boss proudly told my colleague he was out demonstrating in front of our office. But in the same breath he told her he had nothing to do with the protest. We realised why. His was a 'shadow' affair. This was the new face of Indian business—the hidden lobbyist who could skillfully make out cases for clients in different ways, from power-point presentations to physical protest, all on hire, for a price.

Clearly this is now the toolkit of industry to deal with dissent— to suppress public opinion and to subvert decision-making via a fine public relations makeover. If you don't believe me just consider how, in this same period, the pesticide industry through its associations has filed countless cases against activists and scientists, but with an important difference. These cases derive from what is known in the US as SLAPP—acronym for 'strategic lawsuits against public participation'. These are 'different' because the corporation (or its front organisation or lawyer) uses it not to get justice, but to threaten, intimidate and gag. The cases are filed not against institutions that can defend their interests but carefully target individuals and, in particular, professionals who refuse to prostitute their science to suit industry. The companies who file SLAPP cases rarely win in court, but make the defendants spend a huge amount of time and money running to the courts to fight the case. This harassment discourages others from petitioning government on public issues. Industry's business is served.

There was a history to all this. In the early 1960s, the Kerala agriculture department began planting cashew trees on the hills around Padre. This estate was taken over in 1978 by the Plantation Corporation of Kerala (PCK), which soon began spraying endosulfan over the area 2–3 times a year. Concerns sprouted a decade or so later. In 1991, the Union agriculture ministry constituted a high-powered committee to review whether some pesticides, including endosulfan, should be persisted with. The panel recommended the continued use of endosulfan, but cautioned against using it near waterbodies as the pesticide could pollute it, given the fact that endosulfan was known to be toxic to fishes. The panel said this should be put forward as a condition while issuing certificates of registration. In 1999, a committee of the Central Insecticides Board too insisted that labeling in bold letters be made mandatory to avoid usage of endosulfan near waterbodies. Beginning 1997, Mohana Kumar started taking an interest in the subject, and ended up opening the Pandora's box.

Innumerable news reports and field studies built up a case against the malignant effects of endosulfan. On 21 February

2001, CSE published the findings of its pesticide monitoring study report on Kasaragod—high amount of endosulfan residues were found in most of the samples. Two days later, the Kerala government asked its agriculture department to look into the issue. Meanwhile, two studies of the Kerala Agriculture University (KAU) recommended an immediate stop on aerial spraying and called for a need-based application of insecticides. The KAU report also claimed that endosulfan was not likely to have any impact on the human reproductive system and 'did not appear to be carcinogenic,' and that it was relatively toxic to fish but comparatively safe for honey bees.

But when a 23 July 2001 report headlined 'Spray of Misery' in *India Today* magazine documented the physical and mental illness faced by people due to endosulfan, the National Human Rights Commission (NHRC) took *suo motu* cognisance of the issue. It asked the Indian Council of Medical Research (ICMR) for a detailed report, and a three-member team from the National Institute of Occupational Health (NIOH) was constituted.

The NIOH released its findings in two phases. The first instalment, in January 2002, talked of the presence of endosulfan residues in water samples as well as in blood samples from Padre village. It concluded that there was a high prevalence of congenital malformations in exposed groups, low intelligence quotient (IQ), scholastic backwardness, learning disability, early menarche in girls and delayed puberty in boys. The second tranche, released on 24 July 2002, found higher prevalence of neurobehavioural disorder and congenital malformations in females and abnormalities in the male reproductive system in Enmakaje panchayat in Kasaragod district as compared to the control group in neighbouring Meenja panchayat. It concluded that the health problems in Enmakaje was due to the high and continued exposure to endosulfan through various environmental media such as food, water, soil and air.

In between the two reports, an inter-ministerial committee at the Centre sought the view of the Insecticides Registration Committee under the Insecticides Act, 1968. The committee constituted an expert group chaired by OP Dubey, assistant director-general (plant protection) at the Indian Council of Agricultural Research (ICAR). It was meant to examine the innumerable reports on the subject that had been published in the past year or so. The Dubey committee report, released in March 2003, established no link between use of endosulfan in PCK plantations and health problems reported in Padre village. A subsequent committee, headed by agriculture commissioner CD Mayee, parroted the Dubey committee's findings.

In April 2004 and August 2005, *Down To Earth* published exposes on the way the Dubey committee had functioned. The first contended that the panel was manipulated, evidence was suppressed, and facts were distorted to give endosulfan a clean chit. The committee had simply ignored the censorious answers given by NIOH to the queries posed by it. The second article showed how Dubey had suppressed dissent, and that the majority of the scientific members in the committee had ruled against endosulfan. On 13 December 2005, the Union ministry of agriculture issued a gazette notification restricting the use of endosulfan in any form in Kerala. That's when harassment and intimidation started.

A non-profit was propped up under the name of the Centre for Environment and Agrochemicals (CEA), which claimed to work for the welfare of farmers and promoting the judicious use of pesticides. On 3 June 2006, CEA sent a notice to NIOH asking for an unconditional apology in writing and asking it to withdraw with immediate effect a presentation 'Impact of Endosulfan on

Human Health' made by NIOH at a seminar organised by CSE on 25 March. CEA said that the study was unfounded and unscientific. Another notice on 7 September questioned how Dr Aruna Dewan of NIOH lent credibility to the claims of CSE's study on adverse effects of endosulfan usage in Kasaragod. CCFI too sent notices to CSE asking it to withdraw the study. On 30 December that year, CCFI filed a case of defamation against CSE. The NGO responded saying that the study was in public interest and in the public domain and that there was no case of defamation. Meanwhile, CEA filed a defamation case against Dr Dewan in September 2007, and the Pesticides Manufacturers and Formulators Association of India (PMFAI), an institutional member of CCFI, sent a legal notice to Dr Padma Vankar and Indian Institute of Technology (IIT) Kanpur demanding of them to either demonstrate the CSE findings or withdraw the contentions unconditionally.

The harassment did not work, certainly not on the legal front. On 5 January 2008, a magistrate's court dismissed the defamation case filed by CCFI against CSE. The magistrate observed that the report was misunderstood as 'offending.' CCFI challenged the order. On 19 June, the magistrate once again rejected the case, reiterating that the CSE study was not defamatory in nature and that it was merely a criticism.

Even as notices kept flowing, CCFI filed a criminal writ petition against CSE on 10 December 2008. The petition alleged that CSE among other accused had created, printed, published and circulated a defamatory study report on endosulfan with *mala fide* and criminal objective. CSE was made aware of this case on 10 May 2010. The Mumbai High Court rejected CCFI's appeal for expeditious hearing. The next attack came from Excel Crop Care Ltd, one of the largest manufacturers of endosulfan, which served a defamation notice on Sunita Narain and CSE staff involved in the endosulfan study as well as India TV for telecasting a programme titled 'Vishbel', based on CSE's endosulfan study. Incidentally, Excel Crop Care was owned by the extended family of Rajju Shroff, the head of UPL.

India, all this while, unabashedly continued to lobby for endosulfan at the international level much against global trends. First, in March 2010, it blocked for a second time the listing of endosulfan in Annex III of the Rotterdam Convention at the Chemical Review Committee meeting. In October, when the sixth meeting of the Persistent Organic Pollutants Review Committee (POPRC) agreed to adopt the risk management evaluation for endosulfan and recommend listing endosulfan in Annex A of the Convention, a move that would lead to its elimination of the chemical from the global market, India brazenly opposed the move.

Thereafter, the campaign against endosulfan picked up momentum within the country itself. The NHRC, on 18 November 2010, issued notices to the Union and state governments seeking explanations on reports that the aerial spraying of endosulfan in Kasaragod had affected people severely. The following day, the Kerala Pollution Control Board issued a notification to ban any use of endosulfan under the Water (Prevention and Control of Pollution) Act, 1974 and Air (Prevention and Control of Pollution) Act, 1981. The pollution board announced the ban after finding traces of endosulfan in water and sediment samples collected from the Shiriya river and nearby watercourses in Kasaragod. Karnataka, which had been faced with similar endosulfan-related problems in Dakshina Kannada district, banned the chemical in February 2011.

The hard lobbying continued. A farmers meeting, that was ostensibly organised by Excel Crop Care in March 2011, called for a probe by the Central Bureau of Investigation (CBI) on CSE allegedly getting funds from the European Union (EU) to work against endosulfan in India. An industry magazine called *Agriculture Today* made similar allegations against CSE at a press conference that was chaired by, of all people, OP Dubey, who had headed the committee that gave a clean chit to the use of the pesticide.

The month of April 2011 was tumultuous. On 20 April, Kerala's department of health and family welfare released the *Report on Health Effects of Endosulfan and Progress of Rehabilitation Activities in Kerala*. It was a progress report, but three days later a delegation of legislators and ministers from the state met Prime Minister Manmohan Singh urging him to ban endosulfan. The delegates presented a study by the Calicut Medical College that showed the health impacts of endosulfan on villages in Kasaragod. Singh reportedly said he would wait for the ICMR study before taking a decision.

Between 25–30 April, the fifth Conference of Parties (COP5) of the Stockholm Convention was held at Geneva, Switzerland. India this time relented to the listing of the technical endosulfan and its related isomers in Annex A of the Convention. The listing meant endosulfan would be banned globally. While frenetic deliberations were on, the Supreme Court on 26 April admitted a petition filed by the Democratic Youth Federation of India (DYFI) (the youth wing of the Communist Party of India–Marxist) seeking a ban on the production, sale and use of endosulfan. On 13 May, the apex court passed an interim order banning endosulfan.

The pesticides lobby, however, did not give up. Excel Crop Care sent a legal notice to the Calicut Medical College on 20 July 2011 alleging that the findings of the research report *Epidemiological Studies Related to Health in Endosulfan Affected Areas at Kasaragod district, Kerala 2010-2011* was 'scientifically erroneous' and 'fundamentally flawed.' The company had demanded that the college withdraw the study within a week; it didn't. More than 80 countries, including members of the European Union, Australia, New Zealand, several West African nations, the United States, Brazil, and Canada had already banned endosulfan or announced phase-outs by the time the Stockholm Convention ban was agreed upon. India is expected to phase out the chemical by 2017. Till then, the toxic substance remains in circulation.

For CSE, this had not been the first brush with the pesticides lobby. On 5 August 2003, the centre published the findings of its study on pesticide contamination in soft drinks sold in India. CSE found high levels of toxic pesticides and insecticides, high enough to cause cancer, damage to the nervous and reproductive systems, birth defects and severe disruption of the immune system. Soft drink market leaders Coca-Cola and PepsiCo had almost similar concentrations of pesticide residues, the study claimed.

Hours after the report was released, arch rivals PepsiCo and Coca-Cola convened a joint press conference to condemn the report and question the credibility of CSE's laboratory. The cola manufacturers went on a media blitz, and PepsiCo even filed a writ petition in court arguing that CSE was 'a non-governmental organisation having no legal authority or recognition' and therefore, 'the report prepared by a private person does not have any sanctity in law and could not have been binding upon any person, much less the governmental authorities.' PepsiCo asked for directions from the court to stop CSE from publishing statements and to withdraw materials from circulation and from its website.

The explosive report did have its political fallout: for only the fourth time in Indian history, a Joint Parliamentary Committee (JPC) was constituted. The mandate of the 15-member committee was clear: to find out whether the CSE findings regarding pesticide residues in soft drinks were correct, and to suggest criteria for evolving suitable safety standards for soft drinks, fruit juices and other beverages where water was the main constituent. The JPC report, on 4 February 2004, vindicated CSE's findings, and said it was prudent to seek complete freedom from pesticide residues in sweetened aerated water.

One of the positive denouements of the JPC report was the constitution of the Food Safety and Standards Authority of India (FSSAI) in 2006.

That year, CSE followed up on its 2003 study, by testing 57 samples of 11 soft drink brands, from 25 different manufacturing plants of Coca-Cola and PepsiCo, spread over 12 states. The results, announced on 2 August 2006, found pesticide residues in all samples; it found a cocktail of 3–5 different pesticides in all samples—on an average 24 times higher than BIS (Bureau of Indian Standards) norms, which had been finalised but not yet notified. The levels in some samples—for instance, Coca-Cola bought in Kolkata—exceeded the BIS standards by 140 times for the deadly pesticide lindane. Similarly, a Coca-Cola sample manufactured in Thane contained the neurotoxin chlorpyrifos, 200 times the standard. The health ministry constituted an expert committee to look into the allegations two days later. After reviewing all aspects, including methodology adopted by CSE, the committee said the CSE report did not provide details required for the confirmatory interpretation of quantum results and that the residue data reported was inconclusive.

Narain reacted strongly to the clean chit given by the health ministry to the cola companies, 'We are not surprised. This is the same ministry which had blocked the standards for carbonated beverages that had been finalised by the Bureau of Indian Standards from being notified. The health ministry has specialised in setting up committee after committee, without any outcome... This is clearly a convenient ruse for the industry, but it is inconvenient for us and our health.'

This time there was no defamation notice from the cola majors, but CSE did get a legal notice from—you guess it right—CCFI, as if on cue after the health ministry's exoneration. Agrochemicals Promotions Group (APG) and CCFI, claiming to represent more than 200 leading Indian pesticide manufacturers, sent legal notices to CSE, seeking scientific substantiation of how the minuscule levels of pesticide could affect human health. This bit, however, did not make any legal headway.

The problem of pesticides, nevertheless, persisted. In January 2013, a *Down To Earth* investigation found that the central agency responsible for registering pesticides continued to do so without setting the maximum residue limit (MRL), the legal limit of pesticide residue in food based on good agricultural practices. Of the 234 pesticides registered by the Central Insecticides Board and Registered Committee (CIBRC), 59 did not have set MRLs. None of the JPC recommendations were effectively implemented. Besides asking for discontinuing the practice of registering pesticides without setting their MRLs, the JPC had recommended the reviewing of MRLs periodically and prescribing waiting periods for pesticides.

What is very clear from the campaign histories and writings about the harmful effects of pesticides and other toxic chemicals on human health, is that critical reportage has to confront a no-holds barred onslaught from the pesticides lobby. Defamation cases included.

7

An Omen of the Times

Being taken to court by a corporate entity is one thing. But when the corporate entity in question is a monolithic media house, the incident becomes a travesty in SLAPPs.

In a milieu where one sees increasing corporatisation of the media on the one hand and consolidation of corporate structures that own the media on the other, it should hardly come as a surprise when the media starts gunning for one of its own, quite often a puny opponent in terms of both size and stature. This is what transpired as a fallout of the coverage related to the long-running tussle over intellectual property rights between two big media houses—the Financial Times Ltd (FTL) of the United Kingdom, which belonged to the Pearson Group, and the Times Publishing House Ltd (TPH), part of the conglomerate of companies headed by Bennett, Coleman and Co Ltd (BCCL), publishers of the *Times of India* and the *Economic Times newspapers*. Except, that the SLAPP came after almost 20 years into the legal wrangle.

The context to this started in the form of a curtain-raiser written by one of the authors of this book (Paranjoy) for *Mint* newspaper. The article, dated 3 February 2013, served to provide a backgrounder to the Supreme Court hearing on the case the next day. But little was anyone to know at the time that a battle between two newspaper houses would result in SLAPP notices being sent out to unsuspecting victims. The 2,800-plus-word article worked on the assumption that the battle could be reaching a conclusion soon, and that another fortnight later, the dispute was expected to figure in discussions that were scheduled to take place between Prime Minister Manmohan Singh and his British counterpart David Cameron.

The state of affairs was laid out clearly:

To many, BCCL has already won the battle since it has been successful in stalling FTL's attempts to publish a facsimile edition of the *Financial Times* in India.

People familiar with developments at FTL, however, say the UK firm is challenging multiple legal actions brought by BCCL in a determined manner. They claim the Indian media conglomerate's actions are aimed at 'subverting' government policies that have liberalized the working of the country's print sector. These people spoke on condition of anonymity.

What is clear is that irrespective of who eventually emerges victor as and when the set of legal disputes between FTL and BCCL is settled, it will set a precedent for foreign media companies wanting to operate in India. There is a view that no clear winner can emerge from the bruising battle because both sides have already spent approximately ₹30 crore in legal fees over a period of 19 years.

One of the persons at FTL familiar with the developments contended that BCCL's preoccupation with the UK company's newspaper title is 'obsessive' and 'defies explanation' as the Indian media group can neither hope to gain politically nor commercially from its use of the 'Financial Times' title. 'Our (meaning the UK-based FT's) proposed print run in India would be minuscule, while theirs (meaning BCCL's) is already gargantuan,' the person added.

The article had its share of versions of the dispute. Senior advocate Harish Salve, who was representing FTL in the Supreme Court, said that the 'possible' concern of the Times Group was that once *Financial Times* entered India in any form, 'it is the beginning of the end of their so-far successful endeavour of keeping competition at bay.' He also said: 'I have no doubt in my mind that their opposition stems not from any great principle but from some perception of gain—politically or commercially or both.' The chief executive officer of BCCL, Ravindra Dhariwal, declined to engage with the writer, but he was quoted earlier in *Outlook* magazine (6 August 2012) as saying: 'I don't see why this has become such a big issue. We've been using this ('Financial Times') brand name for ages now. As far as India is considered, we own the name FT in India under the PRB (Press and Registration of Books) Act and we don't need to recognise FT UK.'

By virtue of their very nature, intellectual property rights issues often get mired in litigation, and the one between FTL and BCCL was not a regular open-and-shut case.

FTL's claim was that in India, the 'Financial Times' and 'FT' trademarks had been used in newspapers sold and distributed by the UK firm since 1948. However, it was much later in 1987 that FTL finally filed an application for registration of its trademark 'Financial Times' in India. The company's predecessor had adopted the trademark 'Financial Times' in 1888 when the newspaper was first published.

When FTL applied for registration of the 'Financial Times' trademark, it did so under both Class 9 and Class 16 of trademarks; the application for the registration of 'FT' was done only under Class 16. Both trademarks were registered by the Registrar of Trade

Marks under the Trade Marks Act, 1999. Class 9 relates to, among other things, recording, transmission or reproduction of sound or images, while Class 16 relates to, among other things, printed matter. But all this pertained only to the trademark; while the PRB Act, 1867 governs the rules and procedures for the grant of titles with respect to the publication of newspapers and periodicals. So, no publication can be brought out without a title being allocated to it by the Registrar of Newspapers for India (RNI), the authority to do so under the PRB Act.

The seeds of the conflict-to-come were sown in 1993, when the TPH registered 'Financial Times' under the PRB Act, and in 2005 registered the same name under Class 16 of the Trade Marks Act, despite the fact that FTL already had a trademark registration in the same class. Litigation, therefore, was a foregone conclusion. And as irony would have it, the Chennai-headquartered Intellectual Property Appellate Board (IPAB) on 4 April 2012 struck off the trademark registrations of both FTL and TPH for different reasons.

The board said in its order: 'The use (of the trademark) is neither spasmodic, nor is it clandestine, but it is genuine and consistent; maybe a tad exclusive. However, we repeat, there is no evidence of user from 1948. FTL had made its application stating that it had used the mark in India from 1948...(which) has not been proved and, therefore, we have to hold that the mark wrongly remains in the Register (of Trade Marks)...'

The IPAB also noted that TPH had knowledge of FTL's trademark on account of the publicity generated by a conference organised by the UK company in India in 1981 as well as through syndication agreements under which TPH was publishing articles provided by FTL. Evidence apparently pointed to the contention that TPH not only knew about the existence of FTL, but was also aware of its intention to enter India. This matter reached the Delhi High Court, which had earlier stayed the IPAB order.

This conflict couldn't possibly be missing the context: the plans of *Financial Times* to enter India. Those were times when foreign newspapers were not allowed to enter India. In the early 1990s, the *Economic Times* published by BCCL had worked out a syndication arrangement with FTL. The FTL argument, therefore, was that BCCL was well aware of the UK-based newspaper's plans of foraying into the Indian market. Yet, it was BCCL which was part of a lobby that had opposed the entry of foreign investors into India's print industry. Foreign investment was subsequently allowed to the tune of 26 per cent in 2002. In 2004, the Pearson group picked up a roughly 14 per cent stake in the company that published the *Business Standard* and exited the venture four years later. It was said to have held negotiations with the Network18 Group headed by Raghav Bahl to launch the newspaper in India, but the parleys made no headway.

In the meantime, in 2005, the Union government allowed the publication of facsimile editions of foreign newspapers by Indian companies with or without foreign investment. Four years later, the ministry of commerce and industry permitted 'with prior approval' foreign direct investment of up to 100 per cent in printed publications provided the investor was also the owner of the original foreign newspaper which intended to publish its facsimile edition in India. It was only then that FTL incorporated the Financial Times (India) Pvt Ltd, which applied to the information and broadcasting (I&B) ministry for permission to bring out facsimile editions of *Financial Times* under 'Financial Times Facsimile' and 'FT Weekend Facsimile'. The RNI issued title verification letters for these titles in favour of the Indian corporate entity floated by FTL.

This led to another set of legal wrangles. TPH initiated proceedings against FTL, first in Delhi and then in Bengaluru. The Delhi High Court did not grant any relief to TPH, but the Karnataka High Court stayed FTL from bringing out the facsimile editions. FTL then moved the Supreme Court, challenging the stay on the ground that it had no jurisdiction to do so. The turf itself kept changing: in June 2011, the I&B ministry issued guidelines for syndication arrangements for newspapers. That month, FTL entered into a syndication arrangement with the *Indian Express* and sister publication *Financial Express*. TPH instituted legal proceedings against this arrangement as well, and obtained an interim injunction.

A person familiar with the developments at FTL alleged: 'The British publisher is being deliberately precluded from bringing out facsimile editions in India. This is a subversion of government policy. TPH is publishing a spoiler newspaper called *Financial Times* that is distributed in narrow bits of Delhi. But this newspaper is not readily available and TPH is printing the bare number to ensure that the circulation requirements are met as has been laid down by the RNI. It is difficult to fathom why TPH is acting in this way.'

As the *Mint* article reported, it was a dirty game being played out:

This person also claimed that even if the *Financial Times* of the UK is published in India, it cannot pose a threat to BCCL's business daily, *the Economic Times*, which reportedly circulates around 700,000 copies each day.

'The proposed print run of the *Financial Times* would probably be in the region of 15,000 a day and the price of each copy would probably be much higher than the ₹3 per copy charged by the

ET,' he added, further alleging that TPH's legal proceedings were 'embarrassing' the Indian government.

The *Mint* article had an accompanying piece: an interview with FTL lawyer Harish Salve. The well-known lawyer, in a written response to the issue about TPH allegedly squatting on the *Financial Times* title, remarked: 'While I would like to add a caveat that I have been appearing for FT, with all the objectivity at my command, it is my perception that the litigation is contrived and yet another example of how clever 'lawyering' can use Indian courts with their attendant delays to great advantage. It is for this reason that getting caught in the Indian legal system has been always a nightmare for foreign investors.'

Among those tracking the developments was the *SpicyIP* blog. Founded in 2005 by Prof Shamnad Basheer, an intellectual property (IP) academic and consultant, *SpicyIP* blogged on IP and innovation law and policy. By its own claim, 'Through its independent and objective reporting, *SpicyIP* is committed to increase transparency in Indian intellectual property policy and institutions. *SpicyIP* stands for fair, objective and accurate reporting and review of IP and innovation policy developments from India.' The blog had, till this point, published three distinct posts that looked at the IP battle between FTL and TPH. The contentious post of 13 February came more than a week after the Supreme Court hearing that had been the context for the *Mint* piece.

The apex court bench, headed by the Chief Justice of India, Justice Altamas Kabir, had granted adjournment of proceedings in the Karnataka High Court. This order was given so as to ensure that until the appeal before the Supreme Court was heard and until the validity of each party's trademark determined, any related trademark appeal before the Karnataka High Court would remain stayed.

The *SpicyIP* post was heavily linked, as good blogposts usually are, and was a tracker of the legal battle. But there were some passing remarks, those that could easily miss the eye. The one who had blogged was Aparajita Lath, a 22-year-old law student of the National University of Juridical Sciences (NUJS).

The first remark by Lath was:

> This trademark saga throws light on the problems and obstacles foreign companies have to face when trying to enter the Indian market. After the government's green signal in 2009 to foreign direct investment in printed publications, FTL incorporated an Indian entity called The Financial Times (Pvt) Ltd and applied to the ministry of information and broadcasting to bring out facsimile editions of *Financial Times* under the titles 'Financial Times Facsimile' and 'FT Weekend Facsimile'. It is further reported that the Registrar of Newspapers for India issued title verification letters for these titles in favour of the Indian corporate entity floated by FTL.

And the second:

> The effect of this visit [that of the British Prime Minister], such lobbying and the fate of the case before the Supreme Court can be speculated, but what comes out clearly from this 19-year battle is no matter what the effect of the visit, of the lobbying or of the decision, no clear winner can emerge because both sides have already spent, as reported, approximately ₹30 crore in legal fees over a period of 19 years. This also sets a bad precedent for foreign media companies wanting to operate in India.

The law student, on 23 April 2013, received a legal notice from K Dutta and Associates, representing Times Publishing House Ltd, threatening both civil and criminal defamation. According to the notice, the publication of her post 'caused an irreparable injury and loss of reputation' to TPH. The notice said: 'Pursuant to the publication of the impugned article our client has been contacted by several persons, inquiring about the same. Our client has been questioned and subjected to contempt and ridicule and has suffered immense prejudice and loss of goodwill, reputation, standing and goodwill in the industry.' A similar notice was sent to Paranjoy.

Though the original article had been published in the *Mint*, and it had also being summarised in the *SpicyIP* post, legal notices were not sent to the editor, publisher or printer of that newspaper.

Basheer's response to the legal notice was laced with sarcasm, and raised larger issues:

> To begin with, we'll focus only on the 'legal wrongs' outlined in your notice, and not so much on statements that 'shocked' your client or offended their moral sensibilities in any way. After all, if we go down that path, we could send you stacks of material originating from your client that cause the same effect on us, particularly the numerous page 3 images that continue to assault us on an almost daily basis. More importantly, we're certain that your clients are not paying you for any determination of 'shock' value.

He challenged the apparent technicalities:

> You take issue with our statement that the Supreme Court appears to have stayed the Bangalore proceedings in view of the pending Delhi High Court proceedings dealing with the validity of the trademark. You state that the Supreme Court stay of the proceedings did not expressly state anything relating to the Delhi proceedings. This may be so, but we fail to understand how a technical error in this regard amounts to the legal wrong of 'defamation' in that the said statement lowered the reputation

of your client in the eyes of a reasonable public? If the law has changed in this regard, please do intimate us, so that we may notify our readers of this sea change, which has gone unnoticed, without so much as a whisper.

The *SpicyIP* founder wrote about bouncing the issue off *Mint*, 'We've queried the folks at *Mint*, and apparently you've not sent them any legal notice as yet. We can only guess that you're averse to picking people your own size;' and just before concluding, quipped:

> You chose instead to vent your animosity and target an innocent student who penned her piece in good faith and backed it up with very credible sources, including the views of legal stalwarts. We are particularly amused at your allegation that a 22-year-old law student caused 'irreparable injury' and 'loss of reputation' to a powerful media house by highlighting a highly technical trademark dispute of public importance and reflecting on the protracted nature of the litigation. Continue to amuse us, and we may begin to reciprocate.

The blog did not let go at that. T Prashant Reddy, one of *SpicyIP*'s bloggers, summarised it all in another heavily referenced and linked post on 21 May. It carried links to PDF files of both the notice and the response that was sent out by Basheer. *SpicyIP* refused to go down without a fight, and laid out facts: 'Even presuming, for sake of argument, that some facts were wrong in the post, the remedy is to send us a clarification, more so when the party making such an allegation, is a part of a media conglomerate that claims to publish one of the most circulated English papers in not just India but the world. It is not like the *Times of India* has never made an error in reporting and if they were to be sued for defamation every time they made a mistake they would have been bankrupt by now.' The post also linked to articles on the same blog that had commented on instances of inaccurate reporting by the *Times of India* itself.

Reddy pointed out to the irony of it all:

> The most egregious portion of the legal notice however is the threat of criminal action against Aparajita for alleged defamation. Egregious, since this comes from a newspaper. The Editors Guild of India has been campaigning for the abolition of criminal defamation laws because their reporters were constantly being threatened under these outdated laws and yet Times Publishing House thinks nothing of threatening criminal action against a 22-year-old law student.

The irony lay in the fact that the move to have criminal defamation laws abolished was reported in the *Times of India* itself. This hypocrisy of the group was pointed out by the *Hoot* website as well: the hypocrisy over free speech issues and also about not taking on adversaries its own size.

An editorial piece on the site observed:

> The owners of Bennett, Coleman and Co like to sue, or at least send out intimidating legal notices. They do not pick on people their own size unless they feel considerably provoked. When the *New Yorker* columnist Ken Auletta profiled them last October in a piece called 'Citizens Jain' they were not flattered and sent a long threatening letter charging that his article contained many falsehoods and that he had not spoken to their executives. Says Auletta, 'The *New Yorker* assigned a factchecker, with my support, to check my piece and found no falsehoods and noted that I spoke with their top executives. Our lawyer sent a lengthy letter forcefully challenging their claims. This was several months ago, and that was the last we heard.'

And went on to assert:

> Clearly BCCL chose not pursue a litigious route with the *New Yorker* which painted a colourful and controversial picture of the Jains, their media business and the kind of journalism their flagship publication pursues. This shows that even when the company does pick on big publications it eventually backs off.

As the editorial pointed out: 'And among others who have been sent legal notices seeking ₹100 crore in damages are an online publication called the *Weekend Leader* (in 2011) and the *Hoot* (also in 2011). The former for an article it carried related to the Chennai *Times of India's* coverage of the Mullaperiyar dam controversy. The latter for asking how a TV crew from Times Now happened to be present when lawyer Prashant Bhushan was being beaten up in his chamber by goons.'

The *Hoot* was as acidulous, as Basheer had been in his unhallowed response to the TOI lawyers, in concluding: 'The *Times of India* has on occasion mounted an eloquent defence of free speech. It should consider gracefully extending that to its own critics if it is not to be labeled a bully.'

A case in point here was that of the *Mediaah!* blog that shut down early 2005 in the face of a defamation notice sent to its owner Pradyuman Maheshwari. Most of the content on the blog was commentary/opinion, and made no bones about the fact that it was impious in disposition; and of course almost all of the 19 posts that had been put up on the blog had been about the *Times of India*. Maheshwari bounced back later with his own MxM Media website in June 2011, before an editorial stint with the exchange4media group. The tongue-in-cheek nature of the *Mediaah!* posts, that possibly got the goat of their detractors on Bahadur Shah Zafar Marg (sometimes also referred to as the Fleet Street of India due to the presence of the newspaper offices of the *Times of India*, *Indian Express*, *Business Standard* and *Pioneer*, among others), were arguably a reflection of the blogger's own whacky sense of humour: his Facebook bio described himself as 'a beef-eating Maaru married to a beef-eating Jain.' There you are.

The immensely popular *Mediaah!* blog was a virtual one-man show; but *SpicyIP* wasn't. The latter was a quasi-legal blog with a dedicated following in the legal fraternity, and surprisingly very rarely faced SLAPP litigations given the seemingly hostile and potentially treacherous terrain that it treaded. Prior to the TOI incident, it had earlier been sued only once: over two posts made by Shamnad Basheer about pharmaceutical company NATCO regarding the latter's litigation strategy with Bristol Myers Squibb (BMS).

In the first post on 31 July 2012, Basheer had pointed out how NATCO had launched a generic version of BMS's patented drug dasatinib—despite making a denial, on oath, in para 29 of its written statement in the infringement suit, of any intention to launch a generic version of dastinib. Two days later, the writer remarked, 'NATCO admitted (albeit indirectly) that it had lied in its response to BMS's *quia timet* lawsuit,[28] wherein BMS approached the Delhi High Court in 2009, apprehending imminent infringement of its patent covering dasatinib, an anti-cancer drug.'

On 13 August, NATCO sued Basheer, asking for ₹25 lakh in damages. The *SpicyIP* founder responded in his inimical way, which was followed up on the blog with a post by Reddy on 2 September. He raised issues:

---

28 A *quia timet* (Latin for "because he fears") is an injunction to restrain wrongful acts which are threatened or imminent but have not yet commenced.

This lawsuit against Shamnad is nothing short of an attack on our constitutionally guaranteed right to free speech and expression and a blatant attempt to force self-censorship amongst bloggers, newspapers and other members of media. The corporate mentality in such cases is to sue the financially weaker party with a hope to drain them in a legal battle and thereby make an example out of such a party for daring to disagree with NATCO. Even a losing verdict for companies like NATCO is of no consequence to them as long as they can force free-thinkers to self-censor under threat of lawsuits. Their strategy appears to be working since very few media outlets have reported this cowardly lawsuit. And even those that reported it did so rather cautiously without highlighting the free speech issues (with the sole exception of Nick Robinson's post at *Law and Other Things*) which warned of the serious consequences that this lawsuit could have for free speech.

It is not without reason that bloggers have emerged since the mid-2000s as a possible alternative to the mainstream media, which not only crawls when asked to bend, but also desists from going against corporate interests. And in that, analytical and incisive blogging also becomes crucial to the democratic process: when the mainstream media doesn't do its job of questioning the *status quo*, someone else would have to step in. In this light Reddy's concluding remarks might come across as bravado, but is extremely significant in its resolve not to cower down: 'This is not the first time a corporation like NATCO has attempted to muzzle the free press and it is definitely not going to be the last time. Rest assured that we will provide all support to Shamnad to strongly contest this case and defend our right to free speech. The folks at NATCO are seriously mistaken if they think that this will shut us up.'

And of course, it is not that the *Times of India* does not get its own fair share of defamation notices—it does. The most significant of these came in the aftermath of a series of articles that were published by the newspaper starting 18 August 2015. These articles by Josy Joseph were based on a draft report of the Comptroller and Auditor-General of India (CAG) that found various discrepancies in the accounts maintained by electricity distribution companies in Delhi. The same day Mulla & Mulla & Craigie Blunt & Caroe, a firm of lawyers acting on behalf of BSES Rajdhani Power Limited and BSES Yamuna Power Limited (both part of BSES Ltd of the Anil Dhirubhai Ambani Group, ADAG), served a notice of defamation on BCCL. The series of articles containing allegedly defamatory content that was printed in the TOI and carried on its website were titled 'Delhi discoms inflated dues by ₹8,000 crore: CAG', 'Delhi govt representatives in discoms slammed', 'Discom audit: CAG points out conflict of interests in deals' and 'Discoms made money from meters, says CAG'.

The notice contended that the articles allegedly carried 'False, fictitious and unacceptably offending claims, statements and inferences and conclusions' and the reporting was 'actuated by malice and *per se* defamatory.' It also pointed out that the access to the draft report was *sub judice* since an interim order dated 24 January 2014 passed by the Delhi High Court had stated that the final report of the CAG on the subject would not be submitted without the permission of the court. The ADAG companies accused the owners, publishers, correspondent and executive editor of the newspaper of being guilty of contempt of court in addition to having 'breached journalistic standards' by carrying news that was 'sensationalised' to tarnish the 'goodwill' of the client of the legal firm, namely, the corporate group headed by Anil Ambani.

The legal notice was served on Bennett, Coleman and Co Ltd, the owners of the newspaper; Balraj Arora, publisher; Arindam Sengupta, executive editor; and Joseph. At that time, Joseph's official designation was editor–special projects; he subsequently joined the *Hindu* newspaper.

The notice detailed the efforts made by the power companies in reducing 'AT&C' (or 'aggregate technical and commercial') losses and said the names BSES Rajdhani Power Limited and BSES Yamuna Power Ltd carried 'great value and reputation in the world of electricity distribution.' It argued that the reporting in the 'offending articles' is 'in compete disregard of our clients' actual performance and delivery and therefore highly reckless, malicious, negligent and offending.'

In their reply, BCCL and its representatives simply said that the news reports were 'factually correct,' 'based on proceedings before courts' and 'documents received from reliable sources' and were published in public interest. Four days after the series of articles were published, on 22 August, the *Times of India* published another article titled 'No action on draft CAG report' that mentioned the observations of a bench of the Delhi High Court comprising Chief Justice G Rohini and Justice Rajiv Sahai Endlaw. The bench asked the Delhi government not to take any action against the power distribution companies on the basis of the interim audit report unless ordained by the court to do so. The article also stated that the CAG report had alleged that private electricity distribution companies in the national capital had 'manipulated consumer figures' by misreporting the number of meters installed, 'bought costly power, inflated costs, suppressed revenue and favoured their group companies' and 'inflated their regulatory assets by nearly ₹8,000 crore.'

In its reply, BCCL pointed out that 'in the said news reports, we have not taken unilateral views and have published your clients' position *qua* the CAG report. We have specifically stated that 'the companies have, however, denied the report and claimed that it is both incomplete and *sub judice*. It was a different matter that the CAG report had been critical of all electricity distribution companies in Delhi which included Tata Power Delhi Distribution Ltd, besides the ADAG companies.

The BCCL response, therefore, said:

> The report from a constitutional authority that enjoys the highest credibility not just in India but all over the world should be treated with deserving respect. The CAG is not India's government auditor, but is also a member of the UN board of auditors. The CAG's authority, competence and autonomy should and cannot be called to question for private interests.

> There has not been any injunction, restriction or direction by any court of law on the publication of any article on the Delhi power distributor companies and imposing such a ban would be threatening the freedom of press and an assault on democracy. It is not legitimate to claim a right to privacy and confidentiality on the part of the distributor companies when larger public interest is involved. The articles carried by TOI are not personal opinions or allegations but reports based on information received by reliable sources.

On a regular day, this could have been any other routine dispute over publication and interpretation of facts. The numbers attached, however, magnified its significance exponentially. For, along with the demand for retraction of the published material and tendering of an unconditional apology, the ADAG distribution companies made a claim of a monstrous ₹5,000 crore as 'damages for the loss of their reputation and goodwill' that had suffered through the circulation of the 'offending' articles. The amount sought as damages far exceeded the amount in similar defamation notices/ suits made in the past. This made one of the authors of this book

(Paranjoy) remark on the *Hoot*, 'The amounts being sought as damages by corporate entities in India against publications which have allegedly defamed them are reaching stratospheric levels, even if the chances of recovering such sums of money appear rather remote.' Stratospheric indeed—since this was probably the biggest defamation notice served on any news establishment ever in India.

The other entity in this case—ADAG—too has a history of defamation notices/cases. If this one was astronomical in its sheer size, there had been an occasion earlier when ADAG had gone to the extent of obstructing a magazine from publishing an in-depth report that was in the works.

The incident happened in the last fortnight of April 2014 when the editorial team at *Caravan* was putting together the May issue of the publication. It had been decided that the cover story would be on the country's 13th Attorney-General (AG) Goolamhussein Essaji Vahanvati who, at that juncture, had still not acquired the kind of notoriety he subsequently did in the Coal Scam (on alleged irregularities in the allocation of coal-bearing acreages to private companies producing power) that led to the resignation of law minister Ashwani Kumar. Vahanvati was controversial for the advice he had given to the Manmohan Singh government on various legal issues, as well as his personal role in the second-generation (2G) telecommunications spectrum allocation scam which led to a public spat with the disgraced former communications minister Andimuthu Raja. The cover story on Vahanvati was being written by *Caravan's* young staff writer Krishn Kaushik who had spent months speaking to various people who knew Vahanvati. He had interviewed the AG himself as well as his son, not to mention some of his friends, critics and associates.

Even as the cover story, which had been allotted all of 15 pages in the magazine, was being given finishing touches, a letter arrived on the desk of the editor. It was a terse two-page legal notice dated 18 April from Agarwal Law Associates signed by Mahesh Agarwal. After expressing 'concern' for 'our' clients, ADAG headed by Anil Ambani, the notice stated the following in its third paragraph:

> Our clients are shocked to know that your magazine is proposing to publish an article with the sole intention of causing malicious harm and injury. Several individuals have called our clients that they have been approached by your reporters to gather information about our clients' businesses. The tone, tenor and nature of the queries raised and information sought leaves no room for doubt that you have embarked on a vilification campaign of disinformation to cause damage and harm to our clients' business and reputation. It is evident that you are preparing to publish defamatory information concerning our clients' business. It is furthermore surprising that there has been no formal communication from your publication soliciting responses/clarifications from our clients regarding any comments you propose to make about them in your article.

The letter urged the *Caravan* editor to note that ADAG had given the law firm 'peremptory instructions to lodge legal proceedings, both civil and criminal, in the event of your publishing any news or article or material that concerns our clients and is defamatory and/ or malicious.' Even as the magazine was brushing up the article and working on its response to the legal notice, another letter arrived on 22 April. This one sought compliance with the claims made in the earlier letter. Four days later, yet another letter dated 26 April was despatched to the editor and publisher of *Caravan*.

The edition did not stop in its tracks—the magazine went ahead with the story. On 29 April, the May issue of *Caravan* hit the news-stands in Delhi. That day itself, the cover story on Vahanvati was made available to readers on the magazine's website as well.

By then, the story had become topical as the AG's role in the Coal Scam had started hitting the headlines in newspapers and television channels every single day.

The five-segment cover story, 'Inside Man: The Convenient Opinions of Attorney-General Goolam Vahanvati', ran into nearly 11,000 words, and was unflattering. Among others, it reported:

> A few days after Vahanvati's promotion in June 2009, the well-connected journalist Prabhu Chawla, now the editor of the *New Indian Express*, told the lobbyist Niira Radia that Vahanvati was 'an old friend of mine' during a taped phone conversation. 'He is very close to Anil Ambani, everyone knows about it,' Chawla continued. 'Anil Ambani, Nusli Wadia, and our power minister—*kyaa naam hai?*—Shinde, they all went for him for the appointment. (Governor of Karnataka and former Union law minister Hans Raj) Bhardwaj never liked him. Bhardwaj would not have made him the attorney-general *agar* Bhardwaj law minister *hotaa* (if he was still law minister).' (When contacted for a comment, Chawla said Vahanvati was a friend, and declined to be interviewed for this story.)

> A close associate of Anil Ambani acknowledged Ambani's friendship with Vahanvati, but insisted that the two men were not unusually close, and that their acquaintance was of relatively recent vintage—after Vahanvati came to Delhi. Ambani, this person argued, naturally had dealings with many powerful people in government, and had only come to know Vahanvati through Ahmed Patel; Vahanvati, he said, was close with other corporate leaders as well—closer, this person said, than he was to Ambani.

The ADAG angle kept re-appearing:

> When Anil Ambani's name came up—as it inevitably did—in my conversation with Prashant Bhushan, he argued that Vahanvati should have recused himself from any matters involving Ambani

or his companies. 'Vahanvati told me himself that he is a close friend of Anil Ambani,' Bhushan said. He pointed out that Vahanvati continued to give opinions, or appear on behalf of the government, in cases where Ambani's interests were at stake. 'That, itself, is a conflict of interest.'

As also the relationship between Vahanvati and ADAG:

Whatever the nature of Vahanvati's relationship with Anil Ambani, there are at least two cases where Vahanvati authored opinions pertaining directly to Ambani's companies. In these cases, his opinions were both controversial and beneficial to Ambani's interests. The first of these concerned one of the companies implicated in the 2G scandal, Swan Telecom; Vahanvati's opinion forestalled an investigation into the company's ownership patterns, though the CBI later determined it had been set up as a front company for Ambani's Reliance Communications. The second case pertained to the ultra-mega power plant being set up in Sasan, Madhya Pradesh, by Reliance Power.

A story on the Attorney-General is never a run-of-the-mill story. The Attorney-General is the government of India's chief legal advisor who is appointed by the President under Article 76(1) of the Constitution and must be a person who is qualified to serve as a judge of the Supreme Court. The Attorney-General is responsible for giving legal advice to the government; s/he has the right of audience in all courts of India and has the right to participate in the proceedings of Parliament, though not vote. S/he appears on behalf of the government in all cases (including suits, appeals and other proceedings) in the Supreme Court.

Moreover, the Attorney-General can accept briefs but cannot appear against the government, defend an accused in criminal proceedings or accept the directorship of a company without the government's permission. Unlike the Attorney-General in the

United States (who holds a position akin to that of the Union law minister in this country), the incumbent in India is not supposed to be a political appointee. However, this is not the case in actual practice. Every time a new government comes to power, all old law officers resign and new ones are appointed. Vahanvati's actions needed to be probed, and *Caravan* did what the magazine thought to be its job as a watchdog.

In terms of tactics—that of pre-emptive action—it was very much similar to the one that had resulted in Hamish McDonald's *The Polyester Prince* not being published at all. The difference, of course was there to be seen: while HarperCollins had crumbled like nine pins, *Caravan* stood its ground. Anant Nath, the editor of the magazine, did not comment on the incident.

As a magazine that carries in-depth, long-form articles that delve deep, it is not surprising that the *Caravan* often finds itself a target for SLAPPs. The case that had social media blazing for a long time was the concerning the Indian Institute of Planning and Management (IIPM) and its director Arindam Chaudhuri.

In February 2011, Chaudhuri became the subject of a *Caravan* cover story, 'Sweet Smell of Success: How Arindam Chaudhuri Made a Fortune Off the Aspirations—and Insecurities—of India's Middle Classes', written by Siddhartha Deb, a contributing editor at the magazine and university professor based in New York. The profile showed how Chaudhuri built an image for himself and how he ran his educational institution. The article was also to be a chapter in a book by Deb that was also in the pipeline.

Chaudhuri reacted in June, by filing a ₹50 crore suit against the *Caravan* not in Delhi where both the IIPM and the magazine's publisher Delhi Press were based, but 2,200km away in Silchar, Assam that itself was another 300km from the state's capital of Dispur. The IIPM filed the case at the court of the civil judge in Silchar district through one Kishorendu Gupta, who operated Gupta Electrical Engineers in a Silchar suburb, and was the first plaintiff; the IIPM was the second. Gupta was a commissioned agent who worked for the IIPM on a contractual basis. Although Gupta was called a counsellor, a contract between Gupta and the IIPM showed that Gupta was only a recruitment agent who had a commercial interest and was paid for his service on a commission basis.

It was not the *Caravan* and its proprietors alone who were taken to court; the suit also charged Deb, Penguin (the publisher of the forthcoming book by Deb), and Google India (which, the suit alleged, had been 'publishing, distributing, giving coverage, circulating, blogging the defamatory, libelous and slanderous articles'). The civil court in Silchar granted the IIPM a preliminary injunction, enjoining Delhi Press to remove the article in question from their website, *ex parte*, without any pre-hearing notice.

The Silchar court, in its order granting the injunction against the magazine, noted:

> Defendants had written [an] article making false imputations against IIPM institute with false and concocted facts only to cause damage to the reputations, goodwill, education activities of IIPM institute. The said magazine carries and morphed image of Mr Arindam Choudhury [sic]—dean of the Centre for Economic Research and Advanced Studies of IIPM saying him as a magician/soothsayer in an attempt to portray him as a trickster and falsely stated that Mr Arindam Choudhury [sic] has a reputation as a fraud, scamster and 'Jhony come lately' [sic] in order to malign and defame the dean of IIPM and create a negative public image of Mr Arindam Choudhury [sic].

In a statement on its website, the magazine pointed out certain allegations made by the IIPM:

The present campus at Satbari is also not in the city's outskirts nor the road leading to it is dusty. Moreover, the works [sic] 'proprietor', 'small', 'run of the mill', 'outskirts of Delhi' and 'the road is dusty' have been used by the defendants with the aim to malign and defame the heads of IIPM as well as the IIPM institute.

The Supreme Court on 8 August 2011 stayed the proceedings in the Silchar court, responding to a transfer petition that was filed by the magazine. The *Caravan's* argument was that except for one, all parties to the suit were based in or around Delhi. The matter itself had remained pending for almost four years. The case was finally shifted on 12 August 2015 from the trial court at Silchar to the Delhi High Court. While delivering the order on the matter, Justice Madan B Lokur, who was hearing the case, along with Justice RK Agarwal, described the IIPM's suit as a 'bogus litigation.' It was a small victory for the magazine, but was more incriminating for the IIPM. In September 2014, the Delhi High Court had barred the IIPM from advertising itself as a management school or offering bachelor of business administration (BBA) or master of business administration (MBA) degrees since it was not recognised by the All-India Council for Technical Education (AICTE). One of the clinchers for the *Caravan* was that Kishorendu Gupta had in the meantime died.

All this while, the IIPM was also locked in two other legal wrangles: both SLAPPs. In 2005, the IIPM had filed a case against Rashmi Bansal,[29] a blogger at *Youth Curry* and editor of *Just Another Magazine* (JAM), who published an article in print and online questioning many of the claims made by the IIPM in its brochures and advertisements, which highlighted that the IIPM

---

29 Rashmi Bansal is the author of six best-selling books on entrepreneurship: *Stay Hungry Stay Foolish, Connect the Dots, I Have a Dream, Poor Little Rich Slum, Follow Every Rainbow* and *Take Me Home*.

had not been accredited by any Indian government agency such as the AICTE, UGC (University Grants Commission) or under other state acts. The IIPM filed a case against Bansal from Silchar, even though she operated from Mumbai. The IIPM managed to get an *ex parte* order from the court, forcing Bansal to remove the article from the website. The IIPM also filed for damages.

Four years later, *Careers360* magazine, published by Maheshwar Peri, who was also the publisher of *Outlook* magazine, carried an article titled 'IIPM—Best Only in Claims?' that looked into the authenticity of the claims that the IIPM had been making through its advertisements. It found that the IIPM claimed that its students were eligible for MBA degrees from IMI, Belgium, but the NVAO, the Accreditation organisation of Netherlands and Flanders (Belgium), did not recognise IMI. The story also delved into other claims. The IIPM filed a case against the magazine and the publisher in Silchar, and obtained *ex parte* restraint against them. The institute also filed a criminal case against Peri from Uttarakhand (one of the claims and counter-claims related to the IIPM's Uttarakhand campus in Dehradun), which was later quashed by the high court.

The tactics resorted to by Chaudhuri and the IIPM point to the ways and means by which corporates harass journalists and writers. Filing a case in a faraway place is the easiest way to set matters in motion—the process itself is harassment, or even punishment if one chooses to look at it that way. Chaudhuri/IIPM had remained involved in controversies—mostly related to the claims made by the institute; and the recourse that it usually took to was always the legal way, by finding loopholes in the law. In February 2013, Chaudhuri even got a Gwalior court to issue an order directing the department of telecommunications (DoT) to block 78 web links, 73 of which according to him were 'malicious' and 'defamatory.'

One of these pertained to a July 2012 UGC notice which declared that the IIPM was not a 'university' according to Section 2(f) of the UGC Act. The September 2014 Delhi High Court order punctured holes in the IIPM's contentions, and pushed it on the backfoot.

The *coup de grâce* for Chaudhuri and the IIPM came in January 2016, but made news after almost two months. On 19 March, Peri announced in a Facebook post that his legal battle with Chaudhuri had come to an end on 22 January when he came to know that the businessman had withdrawn all legal cases against him. In the battle of attrition, it was Peri who finally won. He had earlier won a number of cases across the country and was said to have spent a fortune (reportedly an eight-figure amount) in the long-drawn war.

The Facebook post recounted: 'I lost count of the number of cases I defended myself against. At one point, there were 14 matters that I was seized of at different levels, in different courts on different counts. When we did carry the series of three articles in 2009, we never imagined the assault would be so severe. I always believed that if I was wrong, I would unhesitatingly apologise and if I was right, it would not be settled or compromised but decided by a judicial order,' and went on to acknowledge, 'But for a supportive boss at *Outlook* [where he had worked earlier], friends, understanding angels and a great mentor, *Careers360* would not have survived the onslaught. It was a battle between David and Goliath. It was just that I was a determined David.'

After a slew of judgments that went against Chaudhuri in 2014 and 2015, the tide turned overwhelmingly against him. In December 2015, a dogged Peri filed a case in the Supreme Court accusing the IIPM of abuse of the judicial process and requesting transfer of the cases surviving in the Northeast. 'We contended that all parties were in Delhi and the subject matter of the cases in Assam had already been adjudicated in Delhi, Uttarakhand and Chandigarh. There were a few cases in Kamrup and the Gauhati High Court, including the ₹100 crore defamation case which was an irritant.'

Chaudhuri had been severely criticised by a number of courts. In its September 2014 judgment, the Delhi High Court had even remarked, 'In our opinion, the aforesaid is clearly a maze created by the respondent no. 4 (IIPM) to entrap students to enlist with it in the hope of acquiring a qualification which the respondent no. 4 (IIPM) is not entitled to confer and thereby enriching the respondent no. 4 (IIPM) to a considerable extent as is evident from the huge expenditure earlier as well as now being incurred by the respondent no. 4 (IIPM) in publicity in print and electronic media.' The Uttarakhand High Court had quashed the case there saying: 'The common expression in a court room is 'Satyameva Jayate'—Truth shall triumph. Truth is also the best defence in a case of defamation. A truth spoken for public good can never be called defamatory.' For some reason, the refusal to see the truth was a result of Chaudhuri's own hubris.

Peri felt it had dawned on Chaudhuri—albeit belatedly—that a fight in the Supreme Court could probably lead to another adverse court order, and it would be curtains once and for all. Peri recollected Subrata Roy and the Sahara India Pariwar being nailed in the Supreme Court (see chapter: *A Story Finally Told*), and revealed that Chaudhuri had in fact been looking for a settlement. Peri sent a message saying, 'Arindam, Please do what is good for you. Don't do favours as I never sought them. That will help you take the right decision. I have fought your cases for six years and will continue to do so. I never seek favours nor am I silent when I am needed to speak up. That is my DNA. For me, this battle is long over. I am only defending myself against your false accusations. I have much work to do and you are nowhere on my radar. The battle with you is long over. If you have learnt anything in the past five years, I am the happiest.'

These were mostly cases where one media house accused another of defamation and resorted to SLAPP tactics over articles or analyses that were not seen as favourable by the first. However, the terrain becomes more slippery when the import of the subject at hand is huge, as it was in the case of what came to be known as the Radia Tapes controversy. The scandal related to the telephonic conversations between Niira Radia, a lobbyist and an acquaintance of telecommunications minister Andimuthu Raja, and with senior journalists, politicians, and corporate houses, taped by the income tax department in 2008–09. The tapes led to accusations of misconduct by many of the people taped. Radia ran a public relations firm called Vaishnavi Communications, whose high-profile clients include Tata Teleservices and Reliance Industries. Almost all those taped or supposedly taped were powerful and influential.

Outlook magazine carried transcripts of the tapes in its 18 November 2010 edition, and was promptly challenged by the Tatas. Ratan Tata, chairman of the Tata group, petitioned the Supreme Court on 30 November seeking relief for the invasion of his privacy on grounds that the leaked tapes contained his conversations with Radia. *Outlook* was made a respondent in the petition, and damages were sought. Since 2010, all Tata companies—nearly 90 in number—have cut off editorial engagements with the group, which included elementary press releases, and terminated all advertising, a substantial source of revenue. Radia too filed a defamation suit against Vinod Mehta, editorial director, in 2012 in the United Kingdom (UK).

In *Editor Unplugged*, the second part of his autobiography

published by Penguin Books India in 2014,[30] Mehta remarked that a suit filed in the UK did cause some 'trepidation' because of the astronomical costs of litigation in that country.

In the chapter titled 'The Ratan Tata Problem', Mehta wrote of how he 'got trapped' in the bitter power tussle between Ajit Kerkar and Ratan Tata, who took over as chairman of Tata Sons from JRD Tata in 1991. When Tata began work, he had to contend with the powerful super-managers within the group such as Russi Mody of Tata Steel, Darbari Seth of Tata Tea and Tata Chemicals, and Ajit Kerkar of the Taj Group of Hotels. Kerkar, who had turned the one-property Taj Group into the country's largest hotel chain, was the last to move out after thirty-seven years with the group when he was sacked in September 1997 on charges of embezzlement. Since it was a 'hot media story,' *Outlook* had covered the tussle between Kerkar and Tata in great detail. Mehta wrote that while Kerkar and his 'camp' spoke to the magazine, Ratan Tata and the group remained 'studiously mum during the whirlwind.'

Sometime after the Radia Tapes transcripts, *Outlook again* published two articles in its 28 March 2011 and 4 April 2011 editions which alleged that the Tatas 'received undue pecuniary advantage' from Arun Shourie in his capacity as minister for disinvestment when the public-sector Videsh Sanchar Nigam Limited (VSNL) was privatised by the Bharatiya Janata Party (BJP)-led National Democratic Alliance (NDA) government in 2002. The stories alleged that the Tatas had retained 733 acres of prime land in Delhi, Chennai, Kolkata and Pune which they got free with VSNL.

Mehta said these stories were the 'tipping point' in his fast-deteriorating relationship with the Tatas. In 2011, Tata Sons filed

---

30 *Editor Unplugged* was a sequel to *Lucknow Boy: A Memoir*, published by Penguin Books India in 2011.

a criminal defamation suit against Mehta and *Outlook* before the court of the additional chief metropolitan magistrate, Mumbai.[31] There was already pressure on Mehta since he felt 'personal guilt' for the loss of the Tata advertisements amounting to almost ₹5 crore annually.

In 2012, after seventeen years at the helm of *Outlook* magazine, he relinquished editorial control in favour of Krishna Prasad. Mehta, 'prodded' by his own management also went out of his way to 'mend fences' with Ratan Tata. He contacted Arun Nanda of Rediffusion, which had taken over from Niira Radia as the group's public relations agency. Nanda never got back to Mehta though he promised to help.

In May 2013, Mehta met Mukund Rajan, who was appointed chief ethics officer and chief spokesperson of the group after Cyrus Mistry took over as chairman. During the meeting, Mehta expressed his distress at the 'estrangement' between the Tatas and *Outlook*, and offered to issue a clarification on the VSNL story and also express categorical regret at its publication. He also suggested that a mutually accepted text could be drafted by lawyers of both parties which could then be printed in the magazine.

---

31 The media-savvy Tatas are not usually known to file SLAPPs. Its most well-known SLAPP case was against Greenpeace India, which it lost. In June 2010, Tata Sons filed a case of defamation and trademark infringement against Greenpeace, asking for ₹10 crore in damages and for a game titled 'Tata vs Turtle' to be removed from the Greenpeace site. In a 35-page judgment on 28 January 2011, Justice S Ravindra Bhat of the Delhi High Court rejected the Tata plea, upholding the right to free speech and legitimate criticism. In the online game, the Tata logo was shown chasing a turtle. The game, which depicted the turtle running away from the logo, was launched in 2010 to spread awareness about the threat which the Tatas' Dhamra port in Orissa (now Odisha) allegedly posed to a sensitive ecosystem as well as the Olive Ridley turtles. The Dhamra Port Company Limited (DPCL), a 50:50 joint venture between Larsen & Toubro and Tata Steel, was taken over by Adani Port in 2014.

Mehta offered this compromise even as a department of telecommunications (DoT) enquiry endorsed the magazine's allegations that the Tatas should have returned the surplus VSNL land to the government when they acquired the company. Rajan never got back to Mehta. In his efforts to get across to the Tatas, he even contacted Raian Karanjawala of Karanjawala and Company, a legal firm advising the group. Mehta knew Karanjawala socially, but the lawyer never got back, even though he too had promised to help. A Tata director told Mehta that Ratan Tata was personally handling the *Outlook* matter and that Mehta would have to get through to the corporate satrap himself to resolve matters. This was never to happen—Vinod Mehta died of multi-organ failure in New Delhi on 8 March 2015 after a prolonged illness.

Incidentally, there is at least one other instance of the Tata group cutting off advertising support over news reports perceived to be of an adverse nature. It was Niira Radia who reportedly persuaded the Tata group to withdraw advertising to a leading financial daily for a while, multiple sources in the newspaper confirmed to the writers of this book. The contentious reports pertained to the Securities and Exchange Board of India (SEBI) finding that former Tata Finance Ltd (TFL) managing director Dilip Pendse had executed 'illegal transactions' in stocks of four firms, including Infosys and the erstwhile Telco. Pendse was removed as TFL chief in 2001 after a company subsidiary made mark-to-market losses; the group filed criminal charges against him. Pendse denied the allegations, but also had to spend time in jail. When the TFL scandal had rocked the Tata boat, it was Radia who had salvaged the group's image in the media.

Meanwhile, instances of SLAPPs as a means to censor journalists and writers abound. There is only one casualty in the bargain—the public's unfettered right to know. That's why this argument keeps recurring through this book: if that right is snatched away, it is democracy that takes the hit.

If one believes in certain core values, one will need to do away all laws and loopholes that serve only that one purpose: to serve a resounding SLAPP on the face of democracy.

8

The Art of Reporting

Not every writing endeavour sees the light of day, for some are aborted prematurely. That's what US-based writer Kevin Maney and his team of researchers found out to their dismay after Maney had completed his manuscript on Shiv Nadar, founder of information technology giant HCL (once Hindustan Computers Limited). The *USA Today* columnist had been commissioned in January 2012 by HCL itself to work on the book, that was to be published around October 2013 by Penguin Books India. In September 2013, however, Nadar pussyfooted out of the project, reportedly on the basis of a technicality. One of the clauses between the writer and HCL was that the manuscript would require the consent of both parties for publication. Nadar did not give his consent.

Yet, when Maney had started work, Nadar had been cooperative and encouraging. The writer and his team spoke to scores of people, from friends and family members to employees and other associates. Nadar was said to have in mind a book like that of Steve Jobs by Walter Isaacson, and was in constant touch with the team, regularly going through the drafts and providing his own inputs. Little news about the canning of the project came out of Maney, bound as he was by a 'non-disclosure' agreement with HCL. Speculation, therefore, was rife once the news of the project's shelving came out in the open in February 2014.

The *Firstpost* website wondered bluntly, 'What is it that Nadar wanted to cover up? Some uncomfortable truths about his company and himself? We would never know. The book could have served as a much-needed history of evolution of the Indian information technology sector.' There could have been a ring of truth here since Maney and his researchers possibly treaded on slippery terrain. One was reported to be the failure of HCL America; another was the way Nadar moved parts of HCL around.

Today, HCL is a $6.1 billion leading global IT enterprise comprising two companies listed in India—HCL Technologies and HCL Infosystems. Founded in 1976, HCL is one of India's original IT garage start-ups. Originally the research and development wing of HCL Limited, HCL Technologies became an independent company in 1991 when HCL Limited ventured into the software services business. HCL Technologies offers services including IT consulting, enterprise transformation, remote infrastructure management, engineering and R&D, and business process outsourcing. By any measure, both Nadar and HCL were worth more than just a book.

According to a person familiar with the goings-on, this was meant to be a balanced biography. The project started as a book documenting the industry through the eyes of HCL, but a few months down the line it metamorphosed into one on Nadar. This worked fine since the folks at Penguin believed that a personal biography was a potential best-seller. But after the draft was submitted in early 2013, the HCL line went silent. A few months later, HCL's legal team implored Maney to destroy the manuscript and all associated and relevant documents. The escape route for HCL had been laid even before the project had taken off, for there was a clause in the original agreement that both primary parties—HCL and Maney—would have to sign off on the manuscript and both would have to agree to its publication; either one could veto. HCL invoked its veto right and wriggled out of the situation. No SLAPPs, no court cases.

All businesses want mileage, but few have the mettle to be transparent.

A senior journalist, who has on a number of occasions been urged to ghost-write or even write authorised biographies of prominent Indian entrepreneurs, divulges, 'Those would have been nice, glossy, shiny portrayals of these companies and people. If I had done that, I would be viewed as somebody who had compromised my independence. I would then have to cut off from writing about those people/subjects. As a ploy, I demanded exorbitant sums of money to do these assignments. Invariably, that sent the book editors and scouts scurrying in the opposite direction.'

It is definitely not easy writing books about Indian corporates, and as she reasons, 'In India, business reporters have to tread carefully because companies and people can block them and not give them access after those critical articles, let alone books. Reporters feel the pressure. And, why is there not a single book on an Indian enterprise that portrays the inside story? Or a good biography of an Indian entrepreneur? But then, it's the same with our politicians, our Bollywood stars, our sports stars. The project has to be 'blessed' by the person in question. The writer is just a notes-taker, providing the protagonist's version of the story.'

As a result, the Indian public remains in the dark about the country's businesses that have made money and earned fame. This senior journalist maintains without reserve, 'None of these great stories will turn into books. Magazine articles will carefully skirt around the mucky bits of the story. The sterile version will be what the world will see. I daresay, even when Indian companies get big enough to take on global rivals, their stories will remain untold.'

Tamal Bandopadhyay, author of *Sahara: The Untold Story*, agrees that corporate reportage is not easy, 'but my personal take is it is less difficult for a journalist to report on a corporate entity than an author writing a book. This is because corporate India takes books more seriously as they feel the books are for posterity, while newspaper reports are perishable. To be sure, if you do solid research and if you are able to support with documentary evidences what you write, you should not be afraid.'

But even if you are not, you can land up in trouble for the wrong reasons. As veteran journalist Darryl D'Monte, former resident editor of the *Times of India* and *Indian Express* in Mumbai, remembers, 'Anil Agarwal (founder of the Centre for Science and Environment) and Sunita Narain were sued for ₹100 crore by none other than the Tatas in 1999 merely for inadvertently illustrating an article about automobile emissions with photograph of a Tata vehicle. A more recent case is that of Keya Acharya being currently harassed by Karuturi Global. I personally haven't had to pull my punches though, in retrospect, it's not as if I've named too many corporates in stories. I think her case may caution other journalists to take cover.'

Acharya did have to take cover, for the process itself is harassment enough. 'When you talk to lawyers, they tell you that the legal process, in instances of such defamation notices at least, becomes a legal case only when the matter actually reaches the court. In other words, it becomes a legal case when the complainant files the case in court. Yet, for the journalist who has received such a notice, the legal system has already begun working. Why? Because if the journalist does not respond to the notice, the complainant can notify the police that the journalist has not responded to a legal notice and he/she can then be arrested. (A senior journalist, now an assistant editor with a magazine in Mumbai, told me that the police came for her with handcuffs because she had not replied to the legal notice sent to her publication.)'

Talking to veteran journalists, one does get the impression that writing about businesses is fraught with consequences. One journalist who has been writing about the business-rights interface, mostly through his column titled 'Root Cause' in the Mint newspaper, is Sudeep Chakravarti. He is the right person to comment on whether Indian corporations have matured in recent times on issues of corporate compliance or issues related to human rights and press freedom, especially since he started the column.

Chakravarti's response is stark and straight on your face: 'Indian companies remain largely immature with regard to compliance issues related to human rights and media freedom. This immaturity derives from both ignorance and arrogance of power. And here, I would like to include within the ambit of Indian companies also those companies that operate in India. Almost without exception, in one way or another they practice what I term corporate social irresponsibility.'

The irresponsibility that Chakravarti alludes to is a recurrent element that emerges through his writings. He elaborates, 'Coca-Cola, for instance, appears to have one set of compliance parameters related to human rights for the United States (US) and quite another for India, as is proven over its handling of the issues of groundwater depletion and pollution in various parts of India. It has taken Hindustan Unilever Limited (HUL) nearly two decades to acknowledge—compelled, among others, by the Madras High Court—in March 2016 that a thermometer manufacturing factory it operated in Kodaikanal actually harmed employees and the environment. When, as executive editor of a publication I ran an article in 2001 detailing deaths and injury to workers, it sent along a former senior journalist who it employed as a senior public relations professional, to rubbish the article and insist it be taken off the website. I politely threw the man out. As recently as 4 August 2015, HUL, through the Twitter handle @HUL_News, said this: 'Safety is our number one priority. Extensive studies found no harm to workers or environment in Kodaikanal.' My query is this: Why be so eager for remediation, why go in for a settlement—which some claim to be very generous—with former workers, if no harm had come to the environment or to the workers? Such examples are legion. Businesses are hard-wired to get away with anything they can, anywhere they can.'

The Kodaikanal mercury poisoning case does serve as a classic example of corporate irresponsibility. A mercury thermometer factory operated by HUL in the hilltown of Kodaikanal in Tamil Nadu was shut down by state regulators in 2001 after the company was caught for dumping toxic mercury wastes in a densely populated part of the town. By the company's own admissions, more than 2 tonnes of mercury were discharged into Kodaikanal's environment between 1984 and 2001, under the blind eyes of the Tamil Nadu Pollution Control Board (TNPCB). A Union government study in 2011 on workers' health concluded that many workers suffered from illnesses caused by workplace exposure to mercury. The company, however, lived in denial, and carried on with its business as usual.

Till, of course, a social media campaign brought the multinational giant down to its knees. A three-minute Nicki Minaj-inspired video by Chennai-based rapper Sonia Ashraf announced that Kodaikanal 'won't step down until you make amends now.'

It was tailor-made for social media, and public mobilisation site
Jhatkaa.org practically took HUL to the cleaners. At the last count,
more than 3.7 million people from 190 countries had viewed
the video, and over 250,000 people had either tweeted or signed
petitions to Unilever CEO Paul Polman. Within a week of the video
going viral, Polman tweeted about his commitment to resolve the
Kodaikanal issue. On 9 March 2016, a settlement between HUL
and 591 former workers at the factory was announced. According
to The Other Media, Chennai Solidarity Group and Jhatkaa.org,
it was public outrage, not corporate responsibility, that prompted
Unilever to do what it had refused to for 15 years.

Three days later, Nityanand Jayaraman of the Chennai Solidarity
Group asked a pertinent question through an article titled
'Unilever Mercury Poisoning Case: Can Corporations Really be
Human?' on Scroll, 'If anything, the belated settlement and what
it took to get here proves that the phrase 'responsible corporations'
is an oxymoron. Over the years, corporations have laid claim to
personhood, and framed themselves as imbued with human
traits such as morality, care for the environment, compassion and
responsibility. Unilever CEO Paul Polman talks about business as
a force of social good. But is there such a thing as a 'good' or 'bad'
corporation? Can a corporation be expected to behave responsibly,
morally, humanely when it also has a statutory obligation to
maximise returns for shareholders, and a fiduciary compulsion
to do so by penny-pinching?' What remained unsaid was that the
mainstream media woke up to the Kodaikanal crisis only after the
rap video had taken Twitter and Facebook by storm.

Harsh words those, but Jayaraman still asserted, 'Truly
responsible behaviour emanates voluntarily. It should not need to
be enforced. But if Unilever is the gold standard in responsible
corporate behaviour, the Kodaikanal experience shows that

responsibility, and even the long-delayed 'humanitarian gesture,' had to be fought for every step of the way.' But as Chakravarti explains, 'Most companies practice what I call brochure-CSR [corporate social responsibility]: they gloss up intent, publish photos of a few schools or clinics they fund, or the planting of a few saplings, funding a trek or two, some executives run the half-marathon in Mumbai, Pune or Delhi. That evidently accounts for good corporate citizenship. That is what the media is fed, and that is what the media largely laps up. Few media organisations have the bandwidth of both courage and deep pockets to publish something adverse against a business, rigorously question a business, and run the risk of advertising being pulled or reduced, or sponsorship for a conference disappear.'

Sometime in 2010, with the approval of the editor of *Mint* the publication where Chakravarti writes a column on matters of business and human rights, and socio-political and security issues in South Asia [it is the only such regular column on the subject in mainstream Indian media], he drafted a questionnaire to be sent to various reporters and editors in *Mint* for them to, in turn, reach companies they interacted with. As Chakravarti was not a *Mint* employee, but an independent columnist and commentator, it was felt it would be quicker to reach these companies through the journalistic network of the publication, with the purpose of his writing and even editing a series on the specific aspect of human rights and corporate social responsibility related to the mining and metals industry. The brief listed major companies and then provided a series of queries (see annexure: *Chakravarti's Questions*). Not a single company responded, and *Mint* couldn't legitimately push beyond a point because they were actually doing it on his behalf, a non-employee.

Recounts Chakravarti, 'It led me to pursue a book project to deal with the matter in my own way—and, significantly, to continue to address such issues in *Mint*. The book from this experience was published in 2014: *Clear.Hold.Build: Hard Lessons of Business and Human Rights in India*. I followed through and provided cases studies of several companies in this aborted questionnaire. To *Mint's* credit, they have excerpted this book, and published several of my columns based on my research for the book. There has never been any pressure to not write a column on a particular company or business stream, or government. This is unusual—and very welcome—in Indian media, a rarity.'

What would also be welcome is a change in corporate mindset, but has Chakravarti seen anything of that sort? 'My column 'Root Cause' has run since August 2009. Since then, and since *Clear. Hold.Build* has been published (and even a previous work of mine, *Red Sun: Travels in Naxalite Country*), I have seen a change. There is now more engagement. I believe it has come about because there is greater awareness of liability, not on account of altruism. As I write frequently, there is today a globalisation of activism and liability that has followed the globalisation of finance, resources and markets. When people see Shell UK being made to pay for environmental and livelihood damages in the Niger Delta in Africa, they begin to open their eyes. (Some, of course, never learn. Vedanta, Essar, Jindal Steel and Power Limited are at the top of that unseemly heap, along with several others—I am sure you have examples of lawsuits, including SLAPP, they have brought to bear, not to mention pressure and litigation by relatively smaller entities: as with the example of the Fomento Group in Goa suing an activist-blogger for 500 crore, and filing the case in the Calcutta High Court.) Anyway, there seems to be a willingness to engage, to learn the hard truths. I am frequently invited to CEO forums, investment summits organised by banks, to business schools that have begun to tackle matters of human rights. Fear of liability and adverse publicity are key drivers.'

But Chakravarti sees this more among 'softer' organisations, if you will, like those in information technology, or FMCG (fast-moving consumer goods) sectors.' He goes on to explain, 'They have relatively lower impact on the environment, on displacement, forced or otherwise, on large populations. They get away more easily by focusing on things like gender equality in the workplace, or workers benefits, because those are relatively easier to handle. Large industries, the messy industries, still continue to be the terrible boys of business, employing everything at their disposal, from using government as an extension of corporate will to push through a project, even if it means harming—sometimes, even killing—the project-affected.'

But who pushes more? Are listed companies more aggressive in dealing with reportage lest such writing affect share prices? Devangshu Datta, a columnist with a focus on financial markets, points out, 'Listed guys have thicker skins. They are more used to being asked critical or semi-critical questions and still maintain a relationship with the media or financial analysts. The listed ones try to implement damage control. The big unlisted guys [like Arindam Chaudhuri and his Indian Institute of Planning and Management, or Subrata Roy and his Sahara India Pariwar] are very knee-jerk in reactions. The big unlisted guys usually also have more to hide if you look at it that way. That is often why they are unlisted.'

Datta, shortly after legal notices were sent to the writers of *Gas Wars*, had written in *Business Standard* newspaper, 'Defamation suits are accompanied by orders to remove controversial content for an indeterminate period, while the case winds through the legal system. Even if the case is dismissed, and the content made freely available again, this means price-sensitive information may be pulled out of the public domain for critical periods. As a result, huge losses could be suffered by shareholders.'

Defamation notices are about money matters, not only because damages are sought in monetary terms, but also because the companies concerned claim that they had suffered financial losses because of the critical writing or reportage. For someone who keeps an eye on the stock market, does Datta think that such writing indeed makes share prices fall, or even plummet? 'Yes, of course it does. To take an obvious set of cases, any negative advisory by a financial trading house (say Goldman Sachs or ICICI or whoever) usually causes a reaction. If the market thinks that actionable evidence is being put into public domain, the reaction can be quite severe. Take a look at brand value for instance in cases like Kingfisher—the airlines was listed and so was United Spirits. Every negative report about the airlines did impact the booze business as well.'

Even though, on the face of it, critical writing or reportage may be about a particular company or even a corporate group, the public remains in the background. In fact, Datta had written in the article, 'There is also the question of public good and the weighing of the interests of different entities. The interests of one entity—say, the promoter of a business—may be hurt by some content being made public. But that promoter's interests could be outweighed by the interests of shareholders and stakeholders in the same business. In corporate defamation cases, the interests of multiple stakeholders and shareholders will always be involved. Reliance and Infosys, for instance, have large shareholder bases. If a defamation case involves a government department or a public sector undertaking like Air India, public monies and/or national interest are also involved. In the case of

Sahara, the para-banking operations were used to raise money from the public at large—again, that means wide public interest.'

So, if public interest needs to be weighed in, how difficult is it now to write or report about corporate entities who can always (and do so probably at an increasing rate now) resort to legal arm-twisting? Chakravarti looks at the bigger picture, 'Legal arm-twisting is not new. A publication or television network with cojones and ethics and relatively healthy finances will stand by its reporter or editor and, with a correct story, face up to a corporate entity. The tragedy of corporate reporting today is that, this seldom happens. Mainstream Indian media is largely compromised by the carrot of advertising revenue and sponsorship, more than the fear of legal action. Even so-called combative publications and television channels have been utterly compromised by, say, sponsorship of questionable businesses for a conference, investment in the media house, and such. Such compromises extend to even blanking out an event adverse to a company or government, or utterly twisting it to suit a sponsor.'

The situation, to borrow a cliché, is complicated. Datta calls a spade a spade, 'India is a crony capitalistic environment. This has to be accepted as a fact of life even though it's morally unacceptable. This means that almost every business needs to please or placate the government at multiple levels. (An IT business with an export-facing orientation is one possible exception but that same company might also be looking for a Smart City contract in which case it needs to interact with the government). That means cutting corners to get past regulations and obviously, a certain type of shadiness.

'The investor has to look for somebody who will deliver returns to minority shareholders despite being shady enough to interact effectively with the government. The analyst has to make that distinction when recommending investments. If you pick up shadiness in your due diligence, is it the sort that will harm minority shareholders or ultimately lead to the group losing value? If not, is it worth reporting?'

As the reporting continues, so do the adverse reactions. Chakravarti, of course, has faced a backlash of sorts with his *Clear. Hold.Build.* He is candid and straightforward, 'I can name media houses, and specific publications and channels who were asked to not review the book, not invite me for discussions related to the book and its subject matter—ironically, at a time when business schools and industry forums were doing precisely the opposite! Tellingly, the book sells briskly.'

Being in the thick and thin of things, Chakravarti offers a perspective, 'I believe that, as media increasingly gets warped, the curvature of its spine is bent to near-supine, or the spine entirely dissolves, there will increasingly be independent researchers, websites, journals, and books dependent on the goodwill of those who still care about ethics and accountability. It is already happening. It will grow, this 'guerrilla' media.'

The Last Word

New York-based press freedom organisation Committee to Protect Journalists (CPJ) publishes an annual report titled *Attacks on the Press*, which documents trends in press freedom violations across the world. The sections on India over the years have pointed out attacks on journalists in conflict areas like the Northeast, Kashmir and Chhattisgarh, and the impunity with which journalists have been killed in India, not as frequently or heavily as in countries like Iraq, Afghanistan, Somalia and the Philippines, but killed nonetheless.

The 2015 edition of *Attacks on the Press* bucked the trend—this time, the section on India was not about killings or other physical attacks, but about Indian businesses exerting financial muscle to control reportage. CPJ's Asia programme research associate Sumit Galhotra, who had visited India a few months earlier to make an on-ground assessment of the situation, wrote in the India section (published in April 2015):

> Businesses are attempting to exert greater control of media coverage in three ways: using their financial power to silence journalists through lawsuits that chill critical reporting, influencing publishing decisions through advertising revenue, and, in some

cases, taking ownership of news outlets to reduce or eliminate editorial independence at the source.

The public relations wings of big companies have always attempted to control media access and guide the resulting message. That is part of their job. In an era of understaffed newsrooms, they have become more crucial sources to reporters who can make quick use of reports organized internally by the companies. PR staffs also arrange interviews with executives and special visits and trips—known in common parlance as press junkets—and provide hospitality and gifts. Such relationships and perks, which are frowned upon in many countries, are less antithetical to the Indian media, where a culture of responsible journalism and ethics has yet to take root, and carry their own potential for abuse.

The second and third ways—of advertisers dictating or manipulating journalistic reportage and increased corporatisation of the media—have been well documented, and there is enough literature available on the two subjects. It was the first—about lawsuits—that was new to the CPJ annual assessment.

What made CPJ look at this aspect specifically were numbers— numbers that were telling in a way:

> There has been a sharp uptick in the number of defamation suits and legal notices threatening defamation, according to a year-end report published in December 2014 by the Hoot. The report documented 21 such instances in 2014, a significant jump from the seven cases documented by the media watchdog group in 2013 and the two cases recorded in 2012.

CPJ executive director Joel Simon later wrote to the authors of this book, 'Being a journalist in India is challenging, and over the years CPJ has documented numerous instances of violence and government harassment. But beyond those familiar threats a new risk has emerged—efforts by corporate houses to silence critical reporting. The number of legal actions against journalists has increased, according to CPJ research. The threat of being sued for millions and getting caught in a long legal battle chills even veteran reporters. But those working as freelancers without the backing media houses are particularly vulnerable. These emerging legal tactics threaten free and independent reporting, which is essential to democracy. There is also a potential ripple effect across the region, particularly in places that look to India as a model.'

Simon tailored his response to the times, 'Prime Minister Narendra Modi swept into power on a platform of advancing development and delivering growth. Journalists in his India should be free to report and examine the various aspects concerning India's development—and that includes big business, their dealings, and operations. As India emerges as a major economic power in an increasingly interdependent world, business reporting is all the more valuable. Attempts by corporate houses to intimidate critical voices deprive the public—in India and beyond—of vital information.'

He was right, of course—for it was this very concern that took roots around the same time and resulted in the scripting of this book. But rising incidence of SLAPP suits, however, was only the symptom—what one realised was that this was not a trend in itself, but the indirect fallout of a number of other trends.

The first of the trends is the ever-decreasing space for both investigative as well as long-form journalism in the Indian print media. This itself is a result of a number of factors: the print media (both magazines and newspapers) is suffering from declining revenues; the balance of power in news establishments is now tilted so heavily in favour of the marketing and advertising departments, that the editorial wings have been left with virtually no power to call the journalistic shots; pressures from both potential as well as current big advertisers ensure that stories that go against their interests are either toned down to the extent of being bland, or nipped in the bud altogether. Look at this issue from the perspective that big corporates today own most of the major media establishments in the country, and serve covertly as bargaining chips for them. What can journalists do in such lugubrious situations? Carrying out the same journalistic endeavours outside the ambit of the mainstream media is one obvious way out.

The second is a logistical trend. Not all stories can be fleshed out in the standard 600–800 words for a newspaper, or in 12,000–15,000 words for a magazine that publishes long-form stories. What does a journalist do when s/he has something that needs to be fleshed out more? Then, there are developing stories that often take years to coalesce. Except for those meticulously following such a story, it is easy for everyone else, especially the general public, to miss the forest for the trees. In such a situation too the bigger story needs to stitch together the composite smaller stories. And lastly, random incidents from across the country often have a common thread running through them. Such stories too need to be woven together to present the larger story to the public. What all these points cumulatively mean is that books provide a larger canvas for a hard-working, well-meaning journalist to paint the bigger picture.

Three recent books provide classic examples of these three factors. Basharat Peer's *Curfewed Nights* is a telling first-hand account of what people in the Kashmir Valley went through in the late 1980s and early 1990s. Sudeep Chakravarti's *Clear.Hold. Build: Hard Lessons of Business and Human Rights in India* wove together a number of stories about the growing discontent over the manner in which governments and businesses in India treat communities and stakeholders. Our own *Gas Wars*, that was in the making for over four years, joined the dots that included the legal battle between the two Ambani brothers (Mukesh and Anil), the falling output from the wells owned by Reliance Industries Limited (RIL) in the Krishna-Godavari basin off the Bay of Bengal coast, and the various policies and decisions of the Congress-led United Progressive Alliance (UPA) government that seemed tailor-made to suit RIL's business interests. Journalistic non-fiction titles that have hit the stands since 2010 are many, and such numbers are growing.

So, while books come with certain advantages for the journalist/researcher wanting to get the big story out to his/her target readers, books in any case have traditionally held certain other advantages. First, there is a propensity among readers to take a book more seriously than a news item or a series of reports. Besides, books by their very nature have a (longer) shelf life—they are not here to go away. This posits the third trend—a book on a contentious subject can be far more damaging for its protagonists than one news item or a series of reports, which are ephemeral by nature. Public memory is short too. In other words, when a journalist brings out a publication that is critical in nature of a corporate, the book is likely to be taken far more seriously, and perceived to be a far bigger threat. A damning report in a newspaper or a magazine too would meet with the same kind of threat perception. Examples of both kinds figure in this book.

Now, conflate this with the socio-political climate that has been prevailing in India since the Congress-led UPA government was re-elected in 2009, and one will get the drift. Plagued by a number of multi-billion scams and hamstrung by unbridled inflation, the UPA's last days were marked by political turbulence. The anti-graft agitation of the India Against Corruption (IAC) resulted in the formation of the Aam Aadmi Party (AAP), but the political capital from the public discontent was reaped by the Bharatiya Janata Party (BJP), which with its partners went on to form the National Democratic Alliance (NDA) coalition government in New Delhi in May 2014 riding on the twin planks of development and Hindutva. The crackdown on dissent that was practised by the UPA in fits and starts, was gradually institutionalised by the NDA.

The suppression of dissent and free expression with an iron hand never augurs well in the long run for a democracy. For that matter, neither in the short run as well. With much of the outrage in public discourse on the dangers posed to democracy being restricted to issues of nationalism and secularism (or, say communalism), lost in the din has been the issue of democracy being undermined in a milieu where critical reportage takes a hit because of SLAPP suits that corporates initiate against writers and journalists.

The acronym SLAPP is self-explanatory: the term means exactly what it spells out as strategic lawsuit against public participation. University of Denver professors Penelope Canan and George W Pring, who coined the term, did not pluck it out from the skies. Their 1996 book *SLAPPs: Getting Sued For Speaking Out* grew out of the university's Political Litigation Project, an inter-disciplinary project of the Department of Sociology and the College of Law, which had been studying and reporting on such lawsuits for more than ten years. Canan and Pring found a pattern and felt there was a need for a new term:

> When we began studying these cases there was virtually no recognition—by the legal profession, courts, academia, government, or the public—of their similarity or linkage. The tendency was (and often still is) to view them as unrelated and to apply

conventional legal labels: a 'libel' case, a 'business interference' case, a 'conspiracy' case. Looking deeper, we found what they had in common: every case was triggered by defendants' attempts to influence government action—the exact activity covered by the Petition Clause of the First Amendment.

This led the two academics to come up with their own acronym to the problem:

> We coined the name 'strategic lawsuits against public participation' in government, or SLAPPs, to call attention to these cases in an emphatic way, to illuminate simultaneously both their cause and effect, and to encourage lawyers, judges, government leaders, and parties to look beyond labels and deal with them as a new, unitary type of litigation. The acronym is now widely used by judges in court opinions, by lawyers and academics, in the media, and even on television's *LA Law*.

The term since has caught on, and so has the concept. Yet, these are still relatively early days for concerted bids in addressing SLAPPs that serve as a specific tool to disrupt the democratic process. In the Australian Capital Territory, the Protection of Public Participation Act 2008 protects measures intended to influence public opinion or promote or further action in relation to an issue of public interest. And the law is clear on the subject, and there's a penalty clause too—a party initiating a proceeding against a defendant for an improper purpose may be ordered to pay a financial penalty to the Territory. In the United States, 28 states, the District of Columbia, and Guam have enacted statutory protections against SLAPPs. There is no federal anti-SLAPP law yet, and there is ambiguity on other counts too since the extent to which state laws apply in federal courts is unclear, and the circuits are split on the issue. This legal gap is said to have encouraged the practice of what is described as 'forum shopping'. Forum shopping is the practice adopted by litigants to have their legal case heard in the courts thought most likely to provide a favourable judgment.

In India, the term SLAPP is more in vogue among those who are either at the receiving end or the ones who fight for such causes in the courts: journalists/activists and lawyers. The first time that the term was used in a court ruling in the country was in course of the judgment that the Delhi High Court had pronounced in the case that was brought upon the *Rajasthan Patrika* by the Crop Care Federation of India (CCFI). The judgment of 27 November 2009 was a landmark one in that sense (see chapter: *Poison All Around*).

Writing about SLAPPs in the Indian context is itself a problematic chore. There's precious little dedicated documentation available, and the subject of SLAPPs often gets drowned in the overall outrage about free speech and defamation. Needless to say, public awareness is nothing worth writing home about yet.

This is exactly why this subject assumes significance, and there's an imperative need for this book to tell the people of this country how certain measures by corporate houses are subverting and hindering the process of reportage and how this, in turn, undermines democratic values and affects their lives too.

It is unfortunate that this needs to be even asserted at all; but since it needs to be, so be it. The fact is that the Press in a democracy exists for a reason, and has a role cut out too for itself: to perform its role as a watchdog of the goings-on in polity and society; and as veteran British journalist Robert Fisk often puts it, to monitor the centres of power. When this power exists in the form of a politician-businessperson nexus, it becomes imperative for journalists to challenge the *status quo*, in the greater interests of transparency and democracy. And when journalists are prevented from discharging such duties, either through legal coercion or even physical, such attacks can only be perceived as an undisguised attempt at undermining democracy.

There are some who shoot the messenger; then, there are those who sue.

The casualty in both cases is democracy.

ANNEXURE I: Feel Free to Publish

In 2014, the Manas Saikia Foundation published *Freedom to Publish*, which sought to give publishers and authors guidance on defamation and other legal provisions that affect freedom of expression. There is no restriction on copying and photocopying as long as due acknowledgment is made. The title, authored by Savni Dutt and Sneha Jain of Saikrishna & Associates, is also available as an eBook on Amazon Kindle, Apple iTunes, Google Play, Kobo and Nook. Published hereunder are some extracts that look at defences against both civil and criminal defamation:

(I) Some points about defamation
- Any individual who has been allegedly defamed has recourse to both civil and criminal remedies in India.
- The primary distinction between an action under civil law and one under criminal law is that 'malicious intent' must mandatorily be proved to establish liability under criminal law.
- The objective behind protection under civil law is protection of a person against any wrongful loss of reputation caused by another person. Under criminal law, protection is provided against defamation because a defamatory statement may

provoke the person defamed into committing a breach of peace.

- In a given case, civil proceedings and criminal proceedings can proceed simultaneously.
- Civil defamation in India is not codified and an individual complaining of defamation may find recourse under tort law. Therefore, an individual looking to restrain a publication from entering the market, or to remove a publication that is already available in the market, would move under civil law.
- Publishers and authors have joint and several liability for a publication.

(II) Ingredients of civil defamation

To prove defamation under tort law, one has to establish the following:

(a) That the work adversely affects the reputation of the person mentioned in the book in the mind of a reasonable member of society. It is a precursor that the aggrieved person has to establish a substantial reputation in India which is capable of being harmed by the defamatory statement.

(b) That the contents of the work enable a third person reading the work to identify the person being defamed.

(c) That there has been publication of such defamatory content. Publication means making the defamatory content known to a third party. Therefore, mere printing of a book/literary work would not amount to 'publication' for the purposes of defamation. A work shall be understood to be published when it is made available to be read by an audience in India.

(III) Defence against civil defamation

Civil defamation is a tortious and common law remedy. Hence, the defences to a civil action for defamation are also based on those recognised under the law of torts. A publisher/author has the following three defences to an action for defamation:

i. **Truth:** Truth of a statement is an absolute defence to defamation. The principle is that the law will not permit a man to recover damages in respect of an injury to a character which he either does not or ought not to possess. The burden of proof, however, shall rest on the publisher/author to prove that the statement is true. Though it is not necessary that the statement is literally true, what is important to be proved is that the statement is substantially true. Thus, to be able to successfully defend an action for defamation on the ground of truth, it is essential for the publisher/author to have sufficient evidence to demonstrate that the statements alleged to be defamatory are factually correct.

ii. **Fair Comment:** The defence of fair comment protects the expression of an opinion. A fair comment is such a comment which is true, or which, if false, expresses the real opinion of its author, such opinion having been formed with a reasonable degree of care and on reasonable grounds. To successfully defend a defamation action on the ground of 'fair comment', a defendant is required to prove that the allegedly defamatory statements are:

(a) the comments/opinion of the author and are not factual assertions,

(b) the comments/opinions of the author with sufficient factual basis, and

(c) the comments/opinions of the author are made in good faith, without any malice.

A publisher/author would lose this defence if it is proved

that the opinion in question is motivated by malice. The defence of fair comment protects a statement that is made honestly, and without wilful misrepresentation or misstatement, for the good of the public. It is important to note that the defence of 'Fair Comment' is strengthened if the publisher/author is able to prove that the allegedly defamatory content is made on a subject which is of interest to the public.

iii. **Privilege:** The defence of 'privilege' contemplates and identifies certain occasions, circumstances or situations when a person's right to free speech outweighs another's right to reputation. The essence of this defence lies in the law's recognition of the need, in the public interest, for a particular recipient to receive frank and uninhibited communication of particular information from a particular source. In other words, law recognises through this defence that people who are merely discharging their duty as per the demands of the situation, occasion or circumstance, should not be vexed with the costs and trouble of defending numerous actions for defamation. Freedom of speech on such occasions, situations and circumstances has to be totally safeguarded. Hence the defence of privilege protects the maker of statements on those occasions which demand that the maker of the statement speaks his mind without any fear of legal actions.

The defence of privilege is of two kinds:

(a) **Absolute Privilege:** The defence of absolute privilege protects false or defamatory statements, even if they are made with express malice. A person defamed on an occasion of absolute privilege has no legal redress, however outrageous the untrue statement which has been made about him and however malicious the motive of the maker of it.

Examples of occasions/instances when defamatory statements enjoy the immunity of absolute privilege are statements made in the course of—

   i. Parliamentary proceedings
   ii. Judicial proceedings
   iii. Military and Naval Proceedings
   iv. State Proceedings (e.g. communications relating to State matters made by one Minister to another or to the Crown, a report made by a Police Officer to a Magistrate under Section 202 CrPC, etc.)

This list is not exhaustive.

   b. **Qualified Privilege:** In cases of qualified privilege, it is not enough to show that the offending statement was false and defamatory; one must also prove that the statement was made with express malice. Therefore, as opposed to the defence of absolute privilege where even malicious statements would be exempt from liability, for a publisher/author to claim the defence of qualified privilege, it must be established that there is no malice in making the defamatory statement.

Some instances of qualified privilege are as follows:

   (1) Communications made—
       (i) in the course of legal, social or moral duty
       (ii) for self-protection
       (iii) for protection of common interest
       (iv) for public good, and
   (2) reports of Parliamentary and judicial proceedings and proceedings at public meetings, etc.

As stated, the list is not exhaustive.

(IV) Ingredients of criminal defamation

Publishers/Authors may be liable for criminal defamation if they make or publish any imputation with the intention to harm the reputation of the person concerned.

Proving the presence of intention to harm a person's reputation is a condition precedent to conclusively establish defamation. Merely making a statement that may be defamatory without intention to harm reputation is not sufficient. The complainant is required to prove that the publisher/author intended to hurt the reputation of the complainant.

The meaning of 'harm' for the purposes of defamation under the IPC is restricted to harm to the reputation only. Moreover, it must be proved that there is harm to the reputation as assessed from the eyes of the recipient of the defamatory imputation. In other words, it is not sufficient that the complainant feels that the imputation is harmful to his/her reputation.

It is important that the person or group of persons allegedly defamed are identifiable. Their identity should be clearly discernible and established from the defamatory content published. Additionally, even when the complaint is by a group of persons, it is necessary that such a group is a distinct and determinate body whose identity is fixed. Therefore, while a determinate group of lawyers can successfully claim defamation against the producers of a movie, the producers cannot be held liable for defamation of all advocates as a class.

The offence of defamation is complete when the defamatory matter is told/communicated to a person other than the complainant. Nevertheless, certain communications will not give rise to claim for defamation, for instance, internal communications in a company, communication between a person and his lawyer, etc., because these do not go beyond the person's professional range. However, in a case where a publisher is not the printer of a literary work which contains the defamatory content, it may be possible to argue that communication to the printer for the purpose of printing the work may also amount to publication of the book and the defamatory content contained therein. Similarly, courts have held that the distribution of a book to retailers may also amount to publication of the book, even if the book is not sold to the public. In such situations, courts have assumed that the intention with which a book is circulated is for a third person to have access to its content, and that for the period that the retailer has possession of the book, he/she may have read extracts of the book complained about.

(V) Defences against criminal defamation

Criminal defamation is actionable under Sections 499 to 501 of the IPC. The defences to an allegation of criminal defamation are listed in the 10 exceptions that have been enumerated under Section 499 of the IPC.

The chances of success of any defences to allegations of criminal defamation depend upon the nature of evidence available with the publisher/author to establish that the publisher/author does not have any criminal intent to defame.

Specifically, a publisher must insist that the author of a literary work must have reliable evidence/sources for any content that may be defamatory to another person. The defences that may be used to avoid liability for defamation depend primarily on the manner in which the defamatory content has been projected and publicised. For example, where the defamatory content is in a book, depending on whether the book is publicised as a fictional work, a piece on history, or a piece of investigative journalism, etc., any or all of the defences mentioned below may be available to the publisher/author.

While there is some overlap between the defences available against defamation under civil law and a complaint of defamation under criminal law, it is important to keep in mind that the defences to a criminal complaint are strictly restricted to the 10 exceptions provided under Section 499. The exceptions of Section 499, IPC must be regarded as exhaustive as to the cases which they purport to cover and recourse cannot be had to the English common law to add new grounds of exception to those contained in the IPC.

First Exception: A true statement made in public good is exempted from liability. Bare truth is not a defence under the IPC. While the bare truth, even if stated maliciously, is a good defence under civil law, the same would not hold ground in a criminal proceeding. The mandate under criminal law is that even if the defamatory statement made is true, there must be an element of public good accompanying the act. This additional requirement of proving public good or public benefit makes it possible to repress the publication of statements which though quite true, are objectionable, whether on grounds of decency, or as being disclosures of State secrets, or as being painful and needless intrusions into the privacy of domestic life.

Second Exception: A comment or opinion made in good faith about (a) the conduct of a public servant while discharging his public functions, or (b) his character as appears from such conduct, is exempt from liability. This exception exempts only such statements regarding the conduct and character related to discharge of public functions by the public servant. It does not cover imputations which have no relation to the discharge of the public function by the public servant. Additionally, it must be proved that the comment published was made honestly and in good faith, warranted by facts, after exercising due care.

Third Exception: Any comment or opinion made in good faith regarding the conduct of a person, or his character as appearing from such conduct, when such conduct touches a 'public question', i.e., a matter concerning the public, shall not be considered defamatory. For instance, if a medical professional makes a comment about the professional conduct of another medical professional. The professional conduct could also include solicitation of patients to the hospital with which the medical professional is associated; the comment would not be defamatory because the hospital in this case is a 'public question'.

Fourth Exception: A substantially true report of any judicial proceedings is not defamatory. While such a comment may be of slight disadvantage to an individual involved in the proceeding, the knowledge of any judicial proceeding is of public interest and thus exempt from liability. However, it is of paramount importance that the report is substantially true. A publisher/author must be in a position to demonstrate the truth of the report to be able to claim exemption.

Fifth Exception: The administration of justice is a matter of universal interest to the whole public.32 Thus, the criticism of the merits of a case which has been decided (and is not *sub judice*) made in good faith is exempt from liability. Additionally, any opinion made in good faith regarding the conduct of parties, agents and witnesses as appearing from their involvement in such a case, or their character as appearing from such conduct, is also exempt from liability. Thus, so long as such opinions and comments are made (a) in a sub-judice matter, (b) fairly and in good faith, and (c) relate to the conduct of party/agent/witness as appearing from involvement in the case, and not otherwise, the publisher/ author would not be liable. While writing the comment/opinion, the judgment of an author may be biased, however, the same is not a reflection on his good faith and therefore, his comments shall be considered fair.

Sixth Exception: This exception allows the public to be able to freely express its opinion on an author's performance which the author submits to the judgment of the public, including the character of the author as evident from that performance. This only exempts expressions which are made in good faith.

Seventh Exception: The exemption under this section is limited to comments/opinions in the nature of censure, expressed in good faith by person A about person B to person C who has any authority, by law or contract, over person B. Such censure must be limited to such conduct of person B in matters to which the lawful authority relates. Therefore, while it may not be defamation for a person to say something about another servant to that person, the publication of the same in a newspaper shall be defamation.

Eighth Exception: To prove a defence under this exception, one must prove that (a) the accusation about the person defamed is made in good faith, and (b) the accusation is made to a person who has lawful authority over the person defamed in respect of the subject matter of the information. This exception protects the disclosure of accusations to persons who, by virtue of their position, have lawful authority to receive such information. For instance, a complaint made in good faith to the police regarding the unlawful conduct of another person or regarding the conduct of a child to his father, shall not be defamation.

Ninth Exception: This exception protects any defamatory imputation made about the character of another in good faith to protect the interest of the person making the statement, or to protect the interest of any other person. The exception would also be available if the statement is made for public good. To illustrate, this exception protects a publisher/author if the publisher/author imputes that an author is dishonest and thus the publisher/author does not wish to engage in business with him.

Tenth Exception: Cautioning a person in good faith against another person shall not be defamation. To avail of this exception a publisher/author must prove that the defamatory content is made (a) in good faith, and (b) for the good of the recipient of the cautionary statements or of some person in whom such recipient is interested, or (c) for the public good. In order to establish good faith and bona fides, where required, a publisher/author must first prove the necessity of making the statement in the particular circumstances; second, that there was no malice; third, that inquiries to the authentication of the information were made before publication; fourth, that the publisher/author acted with care and caution; and finally that there is preponderance of probability that he/she acted in good faith.

ANNEXURE II: Mystery of the Birla Book

It was possibly the first book in India that embarked on the path of investigative journalism. It was also possibly the first to simply disappear from the market, deep into the black hole of history, and become something of an urban legend.

Provocatively titled *Mystery of Birla House*, the book by Prof Debajyoti Burman was about one of India's most politically influential businessmen, Ghanshyam Das Birla. Published by Jugabani Sahitya Chakra of Calcutta on 2 September 1950, the book vanished from the market and was reported to have been sold to the Birlas through a deal possibly in the late 1950s which eventually included its copyright. Very few copies survived, including one preserved in Delhi's Nehru Memorial Library in the 'rare books' section. Burman was a professor of history and culture at Bangabasi College in Calcutta.

One of the authors of this book, Paranjoy Guha Thakurta, was able to procure a copy of this book from Amazon.com, where it was listed under its 'rare books' section. The two-volume *Mystery of Birla House* cost a whopping $220; the fourth reprint of the book from 1958 was originally priced at a princely ₹5. Precious little is remembered about the book, and even less information about the work can be found anywhere, definitely not online. The author, his book and the circumstances that led to its disappearance is worth researching.

Copies of *Mystery of Birla House* were presented to the president of the Indian National Congress (INC) at the Nasik Congress in 1950, 'with the hope that he will hear the tears falling and throw his weight on the side of the masses to save the country from ruthless exploitation.' Burman's pleas possibly fell on deaf ears, if the prefaces to the second (in 1950 itself) and third (in 1951) reprints are anything to go by. The allegations made in the book cannot be verified cursorily, but those seemed to have been based on rigorous documentation and were also heavily referenced. The book did—as might probably have been unthinkable at that time— level serious allegations against the Birlas, known for the proximity to the Congress party, something that pre-dated Independence.

The prefaces to the second and the third reprints are being extracted here. As indicated earlier, there is no way for us to either verify or even contract the assertions made by Burman, but the extracts in themselves tell a story—in many ways the same overall story that *Sue the Messenger* wishes to narrate.

The preface to the second reprint ran like this:

> We are glad to say that the first print [run] of this book has been exhausted in two months. The production of the book was not to our satisfaction and it had many defects. This was inevitable because it had to be prepared and printed under conditions of extreme difficulty, discouragement and risk, and therefore utmost secrecy had to be maintained. Subsequent events have proved that our apprehension was justified.
>
> When we published the Kesoram chapter in our journal *The Jugabani*, our office and residence, the Udayana Press where the Jugabani is printed and the Reproduction Syndicate who prepared

the blocks, were raided by the police and searched. Even the binders were not spared, their place had also been visited by the police.

The West Bengal Government's eagerness to shield the evil doers was palpable through the modus operandi they adopted after the publication. It was clear that their intention was not to stamp out corruption, but to seal off all loopholes so that any further leakage of information about corruption would become impossible.

After publication of this book, the same thing has been repeated. The West Bengal Government have again let loose their police. The residences of a number of Sales Tax officers have been searched. It must be noted here that even the house of Mr NC Roy had not been spared from this official crusade against honesty and integrity. He is still under suspension.

The police had again made its appearance at the place of the writer. We were invited to co-operate with the Government and help them in their investigation. We wanted to know first of all the ground where we could meet the Government in order to help them and what was precisely the investigation about. He said that leakage of official secrets was a serious offence and the source of leakage should be traced. We reminded him that as a journalist it was our moral duty to unearth instances of corruption, get hold of evidences and publish them, and it was our previous and customary right to refuse to disclose our source of information. It was not possible for us to oblige the Government by aiding them in their effort to punish honesty and perpetuate dishonesty. Had the Government acted in a manner that a loyal citizen and a moral being would expect them to do, we would have been only too glad to place our wholehearted co-operation at the disposal of the Government.

In this book we have brought to light an unhealthy association of the Finance Minister, high officials of the Finance Department and the Birla House which has been responsible for the ruthless exploitation of the masses. The book may be compared to a thermometer showing the degree of corruption prevalent in the administration. We must confess that we were surprised to find the Chief Minister, Dr BC Roy, an eminent physician, trying to cure the malady by breaking the thermometer.

The matter came up before the West Bengal Legislative Assembly in its autumn session.

During interpellations, Mr NR Sarkar, Finance Minister, had to admit that the documents contained herein were genuine and his reply amounted to a public declaration that service unto Birlas was public service. The interpellations were fully reported only in the Nation and are given below:

Things relating to sales-tax assessment of the Birla-owned Kesoram Cotton Mills loomed large in the West Bengal Legislative Assembly yesterday (October 4), during the question hours. Answering to prolonged heckling by Congress Member Mr Bimal Coomer Ghose, Finance Minister Mr NR Sarkar admitted in the long run that the tax-assessment case of the firm was suspended.

It may be recalled that some time ago reports, including facsimile reproductions of official documents, were published in weekly magazines of Bombay and Calcutta alleging irregularities in respect of sales-tax assessment of the firm.

Yesterday, the questions and answers were all between Congress members.

Replying to the question put in the name of Mr Satish Chandra Chakravarty asking 'whether there has been any interference with the course of the sales-tax assessment of the firm of Messrs Kesoram Cotton Mills Ltd, for the years ended March 1945 to

March 1948,' the Finance Minister Mr Sarkar said" 'No.'

'Will the Minister be pleased to state if it is a fact that in June 1948, the Commissioner of Commercial Taxes had ordered the officer who was dealing with the above case not to take any further action on the same?'

Mr Sarkar: 'The proceedings were stayed by the Commissioner on the 26th June, 1948, pending enquiry by him into certain allegations against the assessing officer.'

Will the Minister be pleased to state if it is a fact that at any stage of the above case, all relevant files were taken away by the Commissioner of Commercial Taxes from the officer who was dealing with this case and subsequently returned to the same officer with instructions to proceed with it and still later the officer was transferred?'

Mr Sarkar: 'The stay order referred to above was vacated by the Commissioner on the completion of the enquiry on the 6th August, 1948. The Commissioner called for the relevant files in connection with the said enquiry and returned the same to the assessing authority as the say order was vacated by him on the completion on the 7th November, 1949, in the interest of the public service.'

The thread of the issue was then taken up by Congressman Mr Bimal Coomer Ghose.

Mr Ghose: 'Will the Hon'ble Minister be pleased to state (abbreviated WHMPS) if his attention has been drawn to a report in a weekly paper to the effect that both the Finance Secretary and the Finance Minister had interfered with this case in connection with this assessment?'

Mr Sarkar: 'Certainly not.'

Mr Ghose: 'My question is whether his attention was drawn to the report published in the paper that there was interference.'

Mr Sarkar: 'I do not call it a paper; it is a rag.'

Mr Ghose: 'That is not my question whether it is a rag or not. I am not asking for an answer on that question. I am asking whether the Minister's attention has been draw to such a report.'

Mr Sarkar: 'No.'

Mr Ghose: 'WHMPS in view of the fact that the stay order was vacated and that it was sent back to the same officer to proceed with the case, whether it may be presumed that there was nothing against the officer?'

Mr Sarkar: 'Yes.'

Mr Ghose: 'In view of the answer just given, WHMPS as to whether it would not have been desirable that the same officer should have investigated into this case and completed the assessment before he was transferred?'

Mr Sarkar: 'I do not agree.'

Mr Ghose: 'WHMPS what were the allegations against the officer for which proceedings were stayed?'

Mr Sarkar: "I want notice.'

Mr Ghose: 'WHMPS when the assessment of this has started?'

Mr Sarkar: 'I want notice.'

Mr Ghose: 'WHMPS if he has any idea as to how long the assessment has been proceeding?'

Mr Sarkar: 'About two years.'

Mr Ghose: 'WHMPS whether the assessment has been completed?'

Mr Sarkar: 'No, it is still being pursued.'

Mr Ghose: 'How long it will take to finish this case?'

Mr Sarkar: 'It is very difficult to say now.'

Mr Ghose: 'WHMPS what he meant by saying that he (the officer) was transferred in the interest of public service?'

Mr Sarkar: 'What is written is the meaning—in the interest of public service he was transferred because he was for a long time in his post.'

Mr Ghose: 'WHMPS how long this officer was acting in this post? What is the usual period for an officer to be kept in a particular post and when usually transferred?'

Mr Sarkar: 'Generally two to three years when the departmental heads think that he should be transferred.'

Mr Ghose: 'Is there any other consideration excepting the period of service which might come into consideration for a decision of the fact as to when a particular officer should be transferred?'

Mr Sarkar: 'There is no general rule.'

Mr Ghose: 'WHMPS if this particular officer has been suspended?'

The Finance Minister here took quite a long time to answer and Mr Ghose had to repeat it several times. After the question had finally been put on the query made by the Speaker, Mr ID Jalan, the Finance Minister admitted that the officer had been suspended.

Mr Ghose: 'WHMPS the reasons why he was suspended?'

Here the Chief Minister Dr BC Roy came to the rescue of his colleague and said:

'That does not arise out of this question. We are prepared to give you answer for a proper question but not as a supplementary question.'

The book was sent out to many of our leaders at Nasik while the Congress was in session. We did not get any acknowledgement from any one of them but we found Seth GD Birla coming down to Calcutta soon after. He was seen closeted at the Ranjani, the residence of Mr NR Sarkar, with the Chief Minister and Finance Minister for an hour and a half, and the Finance Secretary of the West Bengal Government standing attendance with a big file. The Birlas' anxiety to lose assessments on the basis of their cooked accounts has always been apparent because once the assessments are complete they will be free to destroy their books of accounts and records which contain primary evidences of this sinister case. Frantic efforts are now being made to complete the assessments and special officers have been deputed for the purpose.

We understand that Pandit Nehru has demanded an explanation from Dr BC Roy of the allegations made in this book. Dr Roy has a long association with the Birla House. Mr NR Sarkar, the Finance Minister, was a Director of Orient Paper Mills and the Hindustan Motors for the period to which our story relates. The present Finance Secretary, Mr B Das Gupta was an officer with a salary of ₹750 when he was lifted up and permitted to draw ₹2,750. The present Commissioner of Commercial Taxes, KB Pal Choudhuri's softness for the Birlas is a matter of long standing and has been proved in the chapter on Orient Paper Mills in this book where he obliged the Company by closing the assessment on the basis of an affidavit which one of his subordinate officers, on subsequent scrutiny, declared to be false. The present Assistant Commissioner of Commercial Taxes Mr SK Bose, who holds charge of the Birla file, has been brought to the present post after transferring MR NC Roy. Mr Bose's nephew acts as a junior to the pleader who deals with the Sales Tax cases of the Birlas! Can any sane person believe that any investigation worth the name is possible with the stooges of the Birlas occupying all these key positions? We are encouraged to learn that the Prime Minister of India has not been satisfied with the face-saving explanation submitted by the West Bengal Government and has returned it to them. Any inquiry worth the name ought to be conducted by a public tribunal presided over by a Justice of the High Court.

Dr BC Roy has succeeded in reversing Pandit Nehru's declaration of a general election in this province which he had made after the defeat of the Congress at the South Calcutta bye-election. We shall watch with keen anxiety whether he succeeds in hoodwinking Panditji once again. Exploiters and corrupters of society will get their moral blow if Panditji rises to his full height this time and takes decision worthy of the Prime Minister of India.

We have faith in the future. We remember how the Dreyfus case was taken up by the progressive forces of France, how Emile Zola's stirring indictment *J'accuse* [I Accuse] had thrown the anti-Drefusards into confusion, how he was prosecuted on a charge of defamation and sentenced to a year's imprisonment, and how ultimately, through a tremendous and long drawn public agitation, there was a general distribution of rewards to the innocent and punishment to the guilty. It was a struggle between conservatism and progress, between absolutism and revolution, a battle of dogmatism against criticism, of authority against liberty. The vindication of Dreyfus meant the defeat of forces which were in themselves antagonistic to the Republic. We have made an invasion on the strongholds of capitalism and arbitrary authority. We have no doubt about the future. It may be delayed, but it must come. God sees the truth but waits.

The mills of God grind slowly, yet they grind exceedingly small.

In many ways, *Mystery of Birla House* offers a classic template.

It was an unscrupulous chronicle of crony capitalism (involving India's biggest corporate group of the days immediately after Independence), a sordid tale of tax avoidance and subsequent subterfuge, and a meticulously documented account of what arguably was India's first major scam. *Mystery of Birla House* is also about whistle-blowers and honest officers, and a blackout of the scandal in the media.

It is a story worth digging out all over again.

ANNEXURE III: Chakravarti's Questions

In 2010, with the approval of the editor of *Mint* the publication where Sudeep Chakravarti wrote a column on matters of business and human rights, and socio-political and security issues in South Asia, he drafted the following questionnaire to be sent to various reporters and editors in *Mint* for them to, in turn, reach companies they interacted with. The brief listed major companies and then provided a series of queries:

QUESTIONS FOR *MINT* SERIES ON BUSINESS AND HUMAN RIGHTS (Please feel free to carry through follow-up questions wherever possible. Thank you.)

- TATA STEEL & RELATED VENTURES (ground clearing being done in Kalinganagar, Orissa; and land acquired in Chitrakote, Chhattisgarh)
- ESSAR STEEL & RELATED VENTURES (existing Essar mining project in Bailadila, Chhattisgarh and Essar acquisition of land at Bhansi, between Bailadila and Dantewada)
- VEDANTA Plc & STERLITE INDUSTRIES (Niyamgiri hills bauxite concession in Orissa and alumina processing plant there)

- POSCO (land acquisition currently in progress in Orissa's Jagatsinghpur district plus mining concession near the Orissa-Bihar border)
- ARCELLOR MITTAL (mining concession granted in Karampada area of southern Jharkhand, bordering Orissa; and locations in Karnataka in the Bellary area)
- JSW AND JSPL (THE TWO JINDAL GROUPS—JSW'S project is stalled in Salboni, West Bengal).

The questions were asunder:

1. What are the company/ group's current work in progress and planned mining (extraction) and metals projects in India? And where precisely are these located, and to be located?
2. What is the nature of the MoUs related to these projects?
3. Please detail the land acquisition pattern for these projects. That is, which of these have been, are being, or is planned to be directly acquired from the original owners of the land; and which of these have been, are being, and being planned to be acquired from agencies of the state the project is located in? And, which, specifically, are these agencies?
4. Have all clearances been obtained for the projects? Please detail.
5. Is there a standard, formulated Resettlement and Rehabilitation (R&R) policy, or is it *ad hoc*, varying from project to project? Please share these details, as well as details of actual Resettlement and Rehabilitation work undertaken.
6. What is the company/ group Corporate Social Responsibility (CSR) mandate? Also, please share ongoing and planned CSR activities?
7. What "best practice" examples can the company/group offer for its R&R and CSR activities?

8. Does the company/group hold human rights sensitization programmes and/or workshops for its employees engaged in projects? Please detail.

9. Is the company aware that the projects in Jharkhand, Chhattisgarh, Orissa, West Bengal, Karnataka, Andhra Pradesh (location where relevant) are located in a zone of conflict with Maoist rebels and other extreme leftwing factions?

10. Why has the company gone ahead, or is planning to go ahead, with projects located in a zone of such conflict?

11. Why did not/is not the company/group waited for the conflict to be resolved?

12. Is the company aware that it may be open to legal liability in India and overseas on account of operating in a conflict zone, and thereby laying itself open to charges of collusion with state agencies both for perpetuation of conflict and for civil and human rights abuses?

13. What is the company's view on allegations that local administrations, both civil and police have become extensions corporate will in order to acquire land, enforce land acquisition, and get the project moving at speed?

14. What are the company/group's views on allegations that while some best practices may be applied in operations outside India, within India these operations are tainted with accusations of application of coercion and administrative muscle? Please share/detail.

Not a single company responded to the questionnaire.

Acknowledgments

A book, from the time it is only a set of stray ideas in the mind of the author to finally coalescing into something eminently readable, is made possible also because of the cooperation and contribution of many others. Without those who I mention here, this book may not have seen the light of day.

- Anirudh Bhattacharyya, for suggesting the title for this work;
- Paranjoy Guha Thakurta, for encouraging me to take the lead on this project;
- Charisma Bharadwaj, for going through the first draft and giving me the exact feedback I needed;
- Jyotirmoy Chaudhuri, for facilitating the publishing and production of this book;
- Srinanda Ganguly, for proof-reading the manuscript;
- Manish Purohit of Authors UpFront, for managing the backstage of the show;
- Shamik Kundu of PealiDezine, for working on the cover;
- Rajeev Dhawan, Karuna Nundy, Apar Gupta and Shubho Roy, for showing us around the law;
- Darryl D'Monte, Hamish McDonald, Joel Simon, Tamal

Bandopadhyay, Keya Acharya, Sudeep Chakravarti, Madeline Earp, and Devangshu Datta, for sharing their experiences and opinions with us;

- A number of journalists, who cannot be named, for speaking to us on condition of anonymity.

— Subir Ghosh

About the Authors

Subir Ghosh (www.subirghosh.in) is a Bengaluru-based independent journalist and researcher who started out his career in sales before switching over to journalism in 1991. His first job as a journalist was with the eastern metropolitan desk of the Press Trust of India (PTI) in Kolkata. He joined the *Telegraph* daily in 1994 and was part of the first 'region desk' that was set up in the newspaper to bring out dedicated pages and supplements for the states of Bihar, Odisha and the Northeast. It was here that he developed a keen interest in Northeast affairs and started specialising in the region. He wrote and reported prolifically on the Northeast during his tenure in the daily.

He shifted to New Delhi in mid-1998 and joined the publications units of the leading non-governmental organisation on environmental issues, the Centre for Science and Environment (CSE). During his short stay here, he worked on the fifth edition of CSE's flagship publication, the *State of India's Environment*. He thereafter moved on to the apex body of the hospitality industry, the Federation of Hotels and Restaurant Associations of India (FHRAI), and served as assistant secretary-general in charge of publications. He turned around the staid black-and-white newsletter into a four-colour glossy which broke even within a year. Here, he also brought out a number of research studies on the state of the hospitality industry in India. His next assignment was with leading wildlife organisation, the Wildlife Trust of India (WTI), where he was in charge of communications: handling publications, the website of the WTI and media relations. He was to have a second stint here again in 2009–2010.

In the interregnum, Subir experimented with the online media and launched two e-zines: The Reviewer (one that reviewed books) and Northeast Vigil (one that aggregated news and information pertaining to the Northeast). In 2005, he started a website called Newswatch which collated news about the media industry, press freedom issues and journalistic ethics. The mainstay of the site were micro research studies about how various incidents and issues would be covered in the Indian media. All these studies were appreciated worldwide for their detailed analyses: each story that was selected for a study was assessed, at times, based on more than 100 parameters. He still specialises in Northeast affairs, and has served in the past as an advisory council member with the Centre for Northeast Studies (C-NES).

Subir is the author of *Frontier Travails—Northeast: The Politics of a Mess*, published by Macmillan India in 2001, and has won two national awards for children's fiction (including one titled *The Dream Machine*, co-authored with Richa Bansal, which was awarded a prize for children's science fiction by the Children's Book Trust). In 2014, he co-authored *Gas Wars: Crony Capitalism and the Ambanis* with Paranjoy Guha Thakurta and Jyotirmoy Chaudhuri. The book is regarded as a seminal work on crony capitalism.

His last stint in the mainstream media was with the Bengaluru edition of *DNA* newspaper. Subir is passionate in writing about conflict, ethnicities, wildlife, human rights, sustainable fashion, poverty, and cinema. He blogs at www.write2kill.in, tweets at @write2kill, and keeps writing occasionally for a number of newspapers and portals. Besides his writing interests, he works as a political and environmental risk analyst and editorial consultant with both corporates and voluntary organisations.

* * *

Paranjoy Guha Thakurta (www.paranjoy.in) is an independent journalist and an educator. His work experience, spanning 37 years, cuts across different media: print, radio, television and documentary cinema. He is a writer, speaker, anchor, interviewer, teacher and commentator in three languages: English, Bangla and Hindi. His main areas of interest are the working of the political economy and the media in India and the world, on which he has authored/co-authored books and directed/produced documentary films. He teaches and speaks on these subjects to students, general audiences and also trains aspiring—and working—media professionals. He participates frequently in, and organises, seminars/conferences, He is a regular contributor to newspapers, magazines and websites. He is featured regularly on television channels and radio programmes as an anchor as well as an analyst and commentator.

Born in October 1955 and educated at St Stephen's College, University of Delhi (1972–75) and at the Delhi School of Economics (1975–77) in the same university from where he obtained his master's degree in economics, he started his career as a journalist in June 1977 and has been employed with various media organisations including companies bringing out publications such as *Business India*, *BusinessWorld*, the *Telegraph*, *India Today* and the *Pioneer*. He worked with Television Eighteen (now Network 18) for almost six years between 1995 and 2001 when he anchored a daily discussion programme called 'India Talks' on the CNBC-India television channel. Between 2007 and 2013, he anchored two one-hour-long weekly programmes for Lok Sabha Television (the channel owned and operated by the lower house of the Parliament of India). He has anchored programmes for other television channels. He is (or has been) a visiting faculty member at reputed educational institutions including the Indian Institutes of Management at Ahmedabad, Kolkata, Bangalore and Shillong, University of Delhi, Jawaharlal Nehru University, Jamia Millia Islamia, Lal Bahadur Shastri National Academy of Administration and Visva Bharati University.

Guha Thakurta served as a member of the Press Council of India nominated by the University Grants Commission (UGC) between January 2008 and January 2011. In April 2010, as a member of a two-member sub-committee of the council, he co-authored a 36,000-word report titled *Paid News: How corruption in the Indian media undermines democracy*. He was the founder director of the School of Convergence (SoC), and has been a consultant at the Institute of South Asian Studies, National University of Singapore, making presentations and writing papers on Indian politics. He has been associated with a number of projects of United Nations organisations, including the International Labour Organization (ILO).

He is a director/co-director/producer of number of documentary films. The films, *Idiot Box or Window of Hope* (2003), *Grabbing Eyeballs: What's Unethical About Television News in India* (2007), *Advertorial: Selling News or Products?* (2009), Freedom Song (2012) were all produced by the Public Service Broadcasting Trust. Other films include *Hot As Hell: A Profile of Dhanbad* (2006–07), *Blood & Iron: A Story of the Convergence of Crime, Business and Politics in*

Southern India (2010–11), *The Great Indian Telecom Robbery* (2011), *A Thin Dividing Line* (2013) on the India-Mauritius double-taxation avoidance treaty, *Coal Curse: A documentary on the Political Economy of Coal Energy in India* (2013) and *In the Heart of Our Darkness: The Life and Death of Mahendra Karma* (2013).

Guha Thakurta was one of the first journalists to write about the telecommunications spectrum scandal in November 2007, and was one of the petitioners in the public interest litigation on the subject in the Supreme Court of India. He has co-authored a book with Shankar Raghuraman titled *Divided We Stand: India in a Time of Coalitions* (2007) and written *Media Ethics: Truth, Fairness and Objectivity, Making and Breaking News* (Oxford University Press, second enlarged edition, 2011). He has contributed articles and chapters to books (including *Realizing Brand India* edited by Sharif D Rangnekar; [Rupa, 2005], *India: The Political Economy of Reforms* edited by Bibek Debroy & Rahul Mukherji [Bookwell, 2004] and *Journalism: Ethics and Responsibilities* edited by Seema Mustafa [Har Anand, 2013]). In 2014, he co-authored *Gas Wars: Crony Capitalism and the Ambanis* with Subir Ghosh and Jyotirmoy Chaudhuri.

Paranjoy is currently editor, *Economic and Political Weekly*. He is also engaged in authoring/co-authoring/editing other books and producing/directing documentary films. Besides, he is a partner of Media Network of India, a firm engaged in designing and creation of content for all media, contract publishing, training of media personnel, establishment of radio stations and other consulting assignments in the media.